Centre for Educational Research and Innovation

The Well-being of Nations

THE ROLE OF HUMAN AND SOCIAL CAPITAL

OECD

ORGANISATION FOR ECONOMIC CO-OPERATION AND DEVELOPMENT

ORGANISATION FOR ECONOMIC CO-OPERATION AND DEVELOPMENT

Pursuant to Article 1 of the Convention signed in Paris on 14th December 1960, and which came into force on 30th September 1961, the Organisation for Economic Co-operation and Development (OECD) shall promote policies designed:

- to achieve the highest sustainable economic growth and employment and a rising standard of living in Member countries, while maintaining financial stability, and thus to contribute to the development of the world economy;
- to contribute to sound economic expansion in Member as well as non-member countries in the process of economic development; and
- to contribute to the expansion of world trade on a multilateral, non-discriminatory basis in accordance with international obligations.

The original Member countries of the OECD are Austria, Belgium, Canada, Denmark, France, Germany, Greece, Iceland, Ireland, Italy, Luxembourg, the Netherlands, Norway, Portugal, Spain, Sweden, Switzerland, Turkey, the United Kingdom and the United States. The following countries became Members subsequently through accession at the dates indicated hereafter: Japan (28th April 1964), Finland (28th January 1969), Australia (7th June 1971), New Zealand (29th May 1973), Mexico (18th May 1994), the Czech Republic (21st December 1995), Hungary (7th May 1996), Poland (22nd November 1996), Korea (12th December 1996) and Slovak Republic (14th December 2000). The Commission of the European Communities takes part in the work of the OECD (Article 13 of the OECD Convention).

The Centre for Educational Research and Innovation was created in June 1968 by the Council of the Organisation for Economic Co-operation and Development and all Member countries of the OECD are participants.

The main objectives of the Centre are as follows:

- *analyse and develop research, innovation and key indicators in current and emerging education and learning issues, and their links to other sectors of policy;*
- *explore forward-looking coherent approaches to education and learning in the context of national and international cultural, social and economic change; and*
- *facilitate practical co-operation among Member countries and, where relevant, with non-member countries, in order to seek solutions and exchange views of educational problems of common interest.*

The Centre functions within the Organisation for Economic Co-operation and Development in accordance with the decisions of the Council of the Organisation, under the authority of the Secretary-General. It is supervised by a Governing Board composed of one national expert in its field of competence from each of the countries participating in its programme of work.

Publié en français sous le titre :
DU BIEN-ÊTRE DES NATIONS :
Le rôle du capital humain et social

Reprinted 2001

FOREWORD

This report is a publication of the Centre for Educational Research and Innovation at the OECD. It was co-authored by Tom Healy and Sylvain Côté, with significant input from John F. Helliwell (University of British Columbia, Canada), Simon Field and many other colleagues within the OECD Secretariat.

This report profited greatly from the advice of a wide range of both academic experts and official country representatives at meetings of OECD committees and boards which guided the development of the work. Two outside events were also particularly significant: first, an international symposium organised and co-sponsored by Human Resources Development Canada (HRDC) and the OECD on *The Contribution of Human and Social Capital to Sustained Economic Growth and Well-being* held in March 2000 in Québec City, Canada; second, a meeting of a group of experts on human and social capital who met at the OECD in July 2000 to review the first draft of this report.

The volume is published on the responsibility of the Secretary-General of the OECD.

Acknowledgements

Among the international group of experts who contributed to the report, particular thanks are due to: Gunnar Eliasson (Royal Institute of Technology in Stockholm), Dominique Foray (Université Dauphine, Paris), David Halpern (University of Cambridge, UK), Tom Kellaghan (Education Research Centre, Ireland), Bengt-Aake Lundvall (Aalborg University, Denmark), Peter MacDonagh (advisor to the Irish Prime Minister), Lars Osberg (University of Dalhousie, Canada), Robert D. Putnam (Harvard University, US), Jo Ritzen (Vice-President, World Bank), Tom Schuller (Birkbeck College, UK), Simon Szreter (University of Cambridge, UK), Jonathan Temple (Oxford College, UK), Doug Willms (University of New Brunswick, Canada), Michael Woolcock (World Bank), Jean-Pierre Worms (Centre de Sociologie des Organisations, Paris).

Special thanks are due to Human Resources Development Canada (HRDC), particularly to Jean-Pierre Voyer and Richard Roy, for supporting the project at various stages, for funding the secondment of Sylvain Côté to the OECD secretariat, and for co-sponsoring the symposium in Quebec City in March 2000.

TABLE OF CONTENTS

INTRODUCTION

The role of human capital in supporting economic and social development is a long-standing theme, although there continues to be dispute over its exact significance. Recent years have also witnessed increasing attention to the role of social capital – exploring the idea that social relationships, as well as individual attributes, play a critical role in economic activity and human well-being.

The purpose of this report is threefold: *i*), to describe the latest evidence covering investment in human capital and its impact on growth and well-being; *ii*) to describe and clarify the more novel concept of social capital; and *iii*) to identify the roles of human and social capital in realising sustainable economic and social development. This report is an input to the OECD projects on economic growth and sustainable development. It also builds on the 1998 OECD report, *Human Capital Investment – An International Comparison*.

Chapter 1 outlines the key concerns, trends, concepts and relationships discussed in the report as well as the main questions to be addressed. Chapter 2 considers the definition and measurement of human capital, covering all types of skills and attributes embodied in individuals relevant to well-being. The sources of human capital in families, schools, communities and workplaces are discussed, especially in relation to the distribution of learning opportunities and outcomes across different groups. The chapter also assesses the empirical evidence for the impact of human capital on the economy and society. Chapter 3 addresses the conceptual and measurement framework for social capital, examining its sources and impacts on a broad range of possible outcomes. The potential for complementarity between human and social capital, both from a conceptual and an empirical standpoint, is discussed. Chapter 4 addresses some basic questions about the implications for public policy of the preceding analyses of human and social capital and identifies further research and data needs at the international level. A key consideration is that many actors are involved in promoting and harnessing high-quality investments in organisations, communities and people.

Chapter 1

EMERGING SOCIAL AND ECONOMIC CONCERNS

"Distinctions must be kept in mind between quantity and quality of growth, between its costs and return, and between the short and the long run… "Goals for 'more' growth should specify more growth of what, and for what". Simon Kuznets in *The New Republic* (1962).

This report is concerned with human and social capital, not as ends in themselves, but as resources which can be used to support economic and social development. The purpose of this chapter is to set the discussion of human and social capital in the context of these broader social objectives.

1.1. What are today's governments and societies concerned about?

Governments and societies seek economic growth but are also increasingly concerned about its impact on the natural and social environments. They are concerned about inequality, about the possibility of new forms of exclusion and poverty as the use of technology expands and, more generally, about the quality of life and health of children, the elderly and individuals and groups confronting economic and social disadvantage. Dealing with these concerns is made all the more complex by changing patterns of work, family life and community engagement.

Inclusion and quality of life are major concerns for government and society…

Underlying these emerging concerns are fundamental shifts in values and patterns of social engagement which are occurring in many OECD countries, shifts which may call for a re-appraisal of policy objectives. Many of these shifts point towards greater diversity and more emphasis on self-expression, individual autonomy and responsibility, subjective well-being and quality of life. The World Values Study suggests that beyond a certain threshold of income per capita, increases in subjective well-being diminish for higher income (Inglehart, 1997).

… and important shifts in values and attitudes are taking place.

Many observers have examined the interface between economic progress and social dysfunction – for example, the implications for workers of rapidly changing technology, skills obsolescence, job insecurity and longer hours of work. This report finds no evidence to show that increased economic prosperity has necessarily depleted social capital reserves, but it does suggest a link between some aspects of economic progress and increased stress or loosening of social ties. However new conditions of production and work also give rise to new opportunities which, when seized, may contribute to significant advances in well-being.

Economic and social progress need not be contradictory…

... but we need to be concerned about long-run changes in human well-being, as well as short-run increases in economic output.

Social objectives are broader than immediate increases in economic output because: *i*) the evolution of total, and not just economic, well-being is of importance; and *ii*) the long-term impact of economic, environmental and social trends needs to be factored into any analysis of current policy options. The time dimension is crucial in considering current investment and production patterns and anticipated future downstream impacts, since uncertainty and long gestation periods characterise many public and private policy choices. To bring about higher and sustainable levels of well-being, it is important to understand the impacts of developments in the human and social environments as well as physical and natural ones.

1.2. What is happening in some of these key areas of concern?

Rapid economic growth has reduced absolute poverty...

Recent decades have witnessed large increases in economic output across OECD countries with increases in standards of living and working conditions as well as in health and educational attainment. Although the rising tide of material wealth may not have raised all boats to the same extent everywhere, levels of absolute poverty and deprivation have declined in OECD countries since the 1950s. While economic growth is not the only policy objective, it does provide the resources for tackling social exclusion, poverty and poor levels of health. Following unprecedented increases in economic output, concern is now turning more to the "quality" of economic growth and how to achieve further increases in well-being.[1]

... but well-being is broader than economic well-being...

Figure 1.1 depicts three layers of well-being.[2] Well-being includes economic well-being but also extends to the enjoyment of civil liberties, relative freedom from crime, enjoyment of a clean environment and individual states of mental and physical health. In this vein, Sen (1987) emphasises opportunities or the "social capabilities" of individuals to choose and achieve the life goals that best suit them. On this approach, growth in economic output enlarges the range of

Figure 1.1. **Relationship between human well-being, economic well-being and GDP**

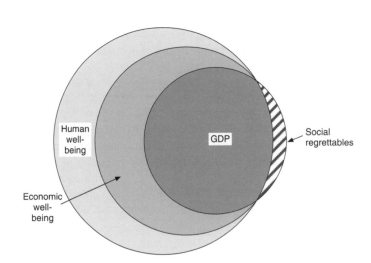

Source: OECD.

human choice (*e.g.* work, leisure or political and cultural activities) rather than serving as a goal in itself. Outcomes ("functionings" according to Sen) are less significant than "opportunities" enabling people to achieve the life that suits them and which they have chosen. The realisation of human capabilities is therefore vital for a broader notion and measure of human and social development. Human well-being is more than the sum of individual levels of well-being since it relates to individual and societal preferences regarding equality of opportunities, civil liberties, distribution of resources and opportunities for further learning.

Economic well-being – flowing from economic output – is an important component of well-being. However gross domestic product (GDP)[3] has significant limitations as a measure of economic output. GDP captures current production of those consumption and investment goods and services accounted for in the *National Accounts* but excludes non-market household activity[4] (such as parenting) and activities such as conservation of natural resources that contribute to future well-being through net additions to the capital stock of society.[5] Aggregate measures of output and income, such as GDP, also fail to reflect social preferences concerning equity goals.

... and economic well-being is broader than measures such as GDP.

GDP includes goods and services which do not contribute directly to well-being. These items are exemplified by so-called "regrettables" arising from outcomes such as pollution, crime and divorce. Figure 1.1 depicts "social regrettables" within GDP but outside well-being (including economic well-being). "Social regrettables" are represented by outlays and expenditures which do not directly contribute to well-being but are nevertheless deemed to be necessary, for example national security (refer to Appendix A).

GDP includes activities which do not contribute directly to well-being.

Our understanding of well-being or human welfare is pervaded by values that will vary between individuals and social groups. There are also technical difficulties in measuring the dimensions of well-being. Subjective aspects of well-being, such as reported levels of life satisfaction and personal well-being, are difficult to measure or relate to underlying explanatory factors.[6] In defining social needs, some judgement is necessary as to how to value the needs of different groups in civil society. For example, a certain degree of income inequality may be desirable for ensuring incentives for work and may also reflect the preferences of individuals for a particular lifestyle, place of living, occupation and balance between leisure and work or between voluntary caring and paid employment. To highlight key social trends, it is possible to choose different indicators and implicitly attach different weights or levels of importance to each (see Appendix A).

We cannot expect a clear consensus on what is meant by well-being...

Despite these difficulties, several attempts have been made to arrive at a summary measure of well-being. One approach (Osberg, 2001) relates to economic well-being only, and brings together four main types of indicators: *i*) current per capita consumption flows; *ii*) changes in capital stocks (including natural and human); *iii*) changes in income distribution; and *iv*) changes in economic risks.

... but this has not prevented attempts to develop summary measures.

Trends in measures of well-being in some OECD countries appear to have lagged behind rising GDP per capita (see Appendix A). Measures by Osberg (2001) suggest that, up to the 1980s, trends in per capita GDP for many OECD countries closely tracked trends in economic well-being, only to diverge since then. The results for 5 countries are shown in Figure A.2. Similarly,

These measures suggest that well-being has lagged behind GDP.

other measures based on a wider range of social indicators (*e.g.* the Index of Sustainable Economic Welfare and the Fordham Index of Social Health) have indicated the same trend since the early to mid-1980s. The main reasons for this divergence were environmental degradation, increased relative poverty and income inequality in some OECD countries.

Economic and social trends are linked, but only partially. Figure A.1 shows trends across a range of social concerns for some or all OECD countries since the mid-1970s or later. These concerns relate to indicators of changes in income, poverty, and labour market participation as well as changing patterns of family formation and health, demography and environmental concerns.

1.3. The inter-relationship between well-being and human and social capital

The role of various factors which impact on well-being as well as their complex inter-relationship is illustrated in Figure 1.2.

Human and social capabilities impact on well-being…
On the "input" side of Figure 1.2 are natural and physical capital as well as "human and social capabilities". Human capital represents the knowledge, skills and health embodied in individuals (see definition in Chapter 2) and social capital refers to the norms and networks facilitating co-operation either within or between groups (see definition in Chapter 3). Political, institutional

Figure 1.2. **Key inputs to human well-being and their inter-relationships**

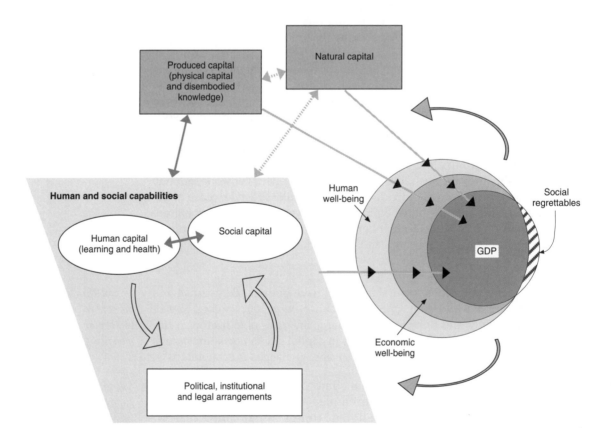

Source: OECD.

and legal (PIL) arrangements interact with human and social capital to influ-ence well-being. Additionally (although to avoid excessive complexity it is not shown in the chart), human and social capital and PIL also have their worn direct links with natural and produced capital.

There is, potentially, a strong complementarity between human capital, social capital and PIL.[7] Coleman (1988), in his work on social capital in the 1980s, stressed the role of strong communities and ties among parents, educators and pupils in fostering learning. On the other hand, education and learning can sup-port habits, skills and values conducive to social co-operation and participation. Good quality institutions, a highly-skilled labour force and the prevalence of norms and networks facilitating social co-operation underpin higher levels of investment in physical capital and can potentially enhance strategies to renew the natural environment. Health is also an important input to well-being and economic performance as well as being linked to age, lifestyle, social status, learning and the extent of social ties and inter-personal support. Indeed, some economists view health as being part of human capital.[8]

... and political, institutional and legal arrangements are extremely important complements to human and social capital.

A range of formal and informal civic, political and legal institutions under-pin market activities and civic life. Institutions set the "rules of the game". Rodrik (2000) describes five types of institutions which:

- Protect private property and contract enforcement.
- Moderate some business activities.
- Support macro-economic stability.
- Provide social insurance or protection.
- Manage social conflict.

Such institutions, when working effectively, can allow countries at different levels of development to handle change and to achieve sustained economic growth.[9]

Closely allied to the concept of social capital is that of social cohesion. Jenson (1998) has defined social cohesion as "the shared values and commit-ment to a community" and has identified five important dimensions: belonging; inclusion; participation; recognition; and legitimacy. More cohesive societies are effective in realising collective goals because they are better at protecting and including individuals and groups at risk of exclusion. Ritzen (2001) states: "The objective of social cohesion implies a reconciliation of a system of organi-sation based on market forces, freedom of opportunity and enterprise, with a commitment to the values of solidarity and mutual support which ensures open access to benefit and protection for all members of society." These understand-ings of social cohesion describe outcomes or states of social harmony, which are the result of various factors, including human and social capital. Hence, social cohesion is a broader concept than that of social capital.

Human and social capital are closely related to the way in which institutions and political and social arrangements impact on society. However, the various elements need to be carefully distinguished, since:

- Human capital resides in individuals.
- Social capital resides in social relations.
- Political, institutional and legal arrangements describe the rules and institutions in which human and social capital work.

Clear distinctions need to be drawn between human capital, social capital and the political, institutional and legal arrangements.

1.4. Is well-being sustainable over time?

Sustaining well-being requires adequate investments in human and social capital...

Some of the effects of human and social capital on well-being take a long time to appear, most obviously the long-term benefits of social investment in children. Inadequate investment might undermine the opportunities of future generations. Consideration of future "social needs" presents a challenge and points to the need for co-ordination across different policy domains. The policy community has increasingly focussed on the importance of sustainable development, reflecting a growing consideration of how environmental policies relate to future needs.

A closer integration of economic, social and natural environment concerns is warranted because of the need to relate long run trends, costs and benefits to present investment choices as well as focus on the interdependence between different processes in any policy consideration. The interim report on the OECD three-year project on sustainable development (OECD, 1999b) stated that "It [sustainable development] has now acquired a broader meaning, implying that the objectives of increasing economic efficiency and material wealth must take into account social and environmental concerns within an overall policy framework".

... since change in both the social and natural environments operate on long-term time scales.

Any degradation of the social environment is likely to occur gradually and affect some groups more than others. This degradation might take the form of increased insecurity, higher incidence of anti-social behaviour including crime, more time spent commuting and lower levels of personal well-being.[10] Some of this erosion, such as declining levels of civic engagement, may not even be initially apparent.

Consequently, social partnership and consensus are important for sustained development.

Social cohesion can mobilise the energy of the population to get things done. According to Rodrik (1998), social polarisation can impair an economy's ability to react to negative economic shocks. An increasing divide between the highly-skilled and the unskilled can undermine social cohesion. Human and social capital can play an important role in facilitating the effective use of skills, the sharing of information and the mediation of conflicts. Dobell (2001, p. 37) notes: "With the resurgence of power exercised through civil society and democratic institutions, economic decisions which have significant distributional consequences cannot be referred to strictly economic calculation nor be determined simply on aggregate cost-benefit analysis or other consequential criteria. Acceptability (legitimacy) in the eyes of an empowered civil society will be essential to social approval for economic action and the pursuit of economic growth."

Notes

1. These concerns are not new. They were evident in the 1970s following unprecedented economic growth in the immediate post-war period. The OECD launched a Social Indicator Programme in the 1970s following a ministerial declaration in 1970 which stressed that "growth is not an end in itself, but rather an instrument for creating better conditions of life" and that "... increased attention must be given to the qualitative aspects of growth, and to the formulation of policies with respect to the broad economic and social choices involved in the allocation of growing resources" (quoted in OECD, 1976, p. 7).

2. Economic well-being is included entirely within "well-being". For the remainder of this report, the term "well-being" denotes human well-being unless the concept is restricted to economic aspects in which case the term "economic well-being" is used.

3. The limitations of existing measures based on GDP were acknowledged by those who contributed to the development of national accounting standards in the mid-20th Century.

4. "The value of women's labor in the home has not been accounted for because it's not part of a market, a mistake worth roughly $8 trillion" (Picciotto, 1998).

5. GDP does include gross investment in physical capital as well as current consumption. However, the contribution of current production to changes in other types of capital stock is generally not accounted for.

6. However, Chapters 2 and 3 will report recent evidence on analysis of reported levels of subjective well-being or life satisfaction which suggest that some of the factors underlying levels of subjective well-being can be identified empirically.

7. In some cases, human capital, social capital and PIL are substitutable as when, for example, formal institutions and rules may substitute for informal social networks.

8. Gary Becker, who was among the first to use the term "human capital", viewed education, on-the-job training and health as components of human capital with consequences for earnings and economic productivity (pp. 54-55 in Becker, 1993).

9. However, as Rodrik stresses, the prescription will vary from country to country as there is no magic blueprint for each and every situation or country.

10. Whether people are less healthy is a separate issue. It may be sufficient for many people to feel that their well-being has declined to signal an issue of concern.

Chapter 2

THE EVIDENCE ON HUMAN CAPITAL

"For growth and prosperity to be sustainable, social cohesion is required; here too, the role of human capital is vital. These tenets are now increasingly accepted" (OECD, 1998, p. 91).

"Education does not have to be justified solely on the basis of its effect on labour productivity. ... Students are not taught civics, or art, or music solely in order to improve their labour productivity, but rather to enrich their lives and make them better citizens" (Weiss, 1995).

2.1. Introduction

Changing economic and social conditions have given knowledge and skills – human capital – an increasingly central role in the economic success of nations and individuals. Information and communications technology, globalisation of economic activity and the trend towards greater personal responsibility and autonomy have all changed the demand for learning. The key role of competence and knowledge in stimulating economic growth has been widely recognised by economists and others.

The economic importance of knowledge and skills is growing...

The non-economic returns to learning, in the form of enhanced personal well-being and greater social cohesion, are viewed by many as being as important as the impact on labour market earnings and economic growth. These personal and social goals of learning are not necessarily inconsistent with the goal of promoting economic performance, not least as well-rounded, flexible and adaptable individuals ready to continue learning throughout life are necessary for realising the economic goals of education.

... while the social impact of learning is just as significant as the economic one.

This chapter seeks to define and illustrate human capital, and to explore its relevance to some key policy issues, including:

- "What works" in promoting effective learning outcomes (section 2.4).
- The impact of different types of learning (level, skill domain or type) on growth in GDP (sections 2.7 and 2.8).
- The question of whether there is under-investment in human capital because some of the social benefits are not captured by individuals undertaking investment.
- The impacts of learning and education on well-being (sections 2.7 and 2.8).

2.2. What do we mean by human capital?

Economists have traditionally identified three factors of production: land, labour and physical capital. Beginning in the early 1960s, increasing attention was paid to the quality of labour, particularly the level of education and training in the workforce. This gave rise to the concept of human capital

Human capital is defined by individually possessed knowledge and skills...

embodying skills and other attributes of individuals, which confer a range of personal, economic and social benefits. Skills and competencies are largely acquired through learning and experience but may also reflect innate capacities. Some aspects of motivation and behaviour, as well as attributes such as the physical, emotional and mental health of individuals are also regarded as human capital. The definition of human capital used in this report is:

The knowledge, skills, competencies and attributes embodied in individuals that facilitate the creation of personal, social and economic well-being.

... and attributes.   While "human capital" has often been defined and measured with reference to acquired cognitive skills and explicit knowledge, a broader notion of human capital, including attributes, more adequately reflects how various non-cognitive skills and other attributes contribute to well-being and can be influenced and changed by the external environment including learning. Human capital is developed in specific cultural settings.[1]

Learning is lifelong and lifewide...   Learning and acquisition of skills and knowledge takes place from birth to death. The concept of lifelong learning emphasises not just the importance of adult learning and training, but also learning at all stages of life including "learning to learn" in the context of schools and other institutions of formal education: both the lifelong and "lifewide". Human capital is developed in the contexts of:

- Learning, within family and early childcare settings.
- Formal education and training including early childhood, school-based compulsory education, post-compulsory vocational or general education, tertiary education, public labour market training, adult education, etc.
- Workplace training as well as informed learning at work through specific activities such as research and innovation or participation in various professional networks.
- Informal learning "on-the-job" and in daily living and civic participation.

This inclusive approach to human capital helps to rebut the criticism that the notion of human capital dehumanises by likening people to physical mechanisms. By contrast, the 1998 OECD report on human capital argued that the concept of human capital "powerfully emphasises how important people have become, in knowledge- and competence-based economies".

... and human capital is multi-faceted...   Human capital is multi-faceted in its nature. Skills and competencies may be general (like the capacity to read, write and speak), or highly specific and more or less appropriate in different contexts. Firm-specific skills and knowledge are acquired through learning on the job and firm-based training. Much knowledge and skill is tacit rather than codified and documented – either because it defies codification, or the task of codification has simply not been carried out. The more knowledge is tacit rather than explicit, the more difficult it is to share and communicate. Lundvall and Johnson (1994) classify knowledge into four categories:

1. *Know-what*: refers to knowledge about "facts".
2. *Know-why*: refers to knowledge about principles and laws in nature, human mind and society.
3. *Know-how*: refers to skills (*i.e.* ability to do something).

4. *Know-who*: involves the social ability to co-operate and communicate with different kinds of people and experts.

Unlike physical capital, human capital is embodied in individuals.[2] Human capital grows through use and experience, both inside and outside employment, as well as through informal and formal learning, but human capital also tends to depreciate through lack of use. Some skills will decline with age and this process partly explains the observed decline in measured human capital (or at least additional earnings associated with any given level of education) beyond a certain age (Mincer, 1974). Hence, human capital cannot be conceptualised as homogeneous and static bundles of skills or competence acquired once and for all by individuals. Some key skills and personal attributes relevant to human capital may be categorised as follows:

... including qualities ranging from literacy to perseverance.

1. Communication (including foreign language competence in each of the items directly below)
   - Listening
   - Speaking
   - Reading
   - Writing
2. Numeracy
3. Intra-personal skills
   - Motivation/perseverance
   - "Learning to learn" and self-discipline (including self-directed learning strategies)
   - Capacity to make judgements based on a relevant set of ethical values and goals in life
4. Inter-personal skills
   - Teamwork
   - Leadership
5. Other skills and attributes (relevant to many areas above)
   - Facility in using information and communications technology
   - Tacit knowledge
   - Problem-solving (also embedded in other types of skills)
   - Physical attributes and dexterity

Fukuyama (1995) notes that "virtually all economic activity... is carried out not by individuals but by organisations that require a high degree of social co-operation". "Organisational capital" reflects the shared knowledge, teamwork and norms of behaviour and interaction within organisations; it is an organisation-level version of the social capital discussed in the following chapter. Leana and Van Buren (1999) define organisational capital as "a resource reflecting the character of social relations within the firm". It is developed through "members' levels of collective goal orientation and shared trust, which create value by facilitating successful collective action". Co-operative effort is encouraged when organisational factors attenuate opportunism, foster trust, encourage open communication, and promote common purposes and values (*e.g.* Axelrod, 1984).

In practice most human activities require teamwork.

Knowledge and networks have assumed an increasingly important role.

There is growing recognition that the management and sharing of knowledge may be central to what has been termed a "new economy" based on fundamentally new organisational and technological conditions (Lesser, 2000). The roles of knowledge, flexibility, trust and networking take on added importance in the search for new ideas and practices in a rapidly changing economic environment. Many observers have linked the concept of the "new economy" to that of a "learning economy", where the capacity of networks, firms and individuals to learn, change and communicate and apply knowledge is qualitatively more important than before (OECD, 2000a).

2.3. How do we measure human capital?

Qualification measures are a simple but weak proxy for human capital.

Educational credentials are a simple and readily measured proxy for skills and competence. Their drawback is that they do not reflect human capital obtained through informal training or through experience, and different educational credentials (for example from different countries) can be difficult to compare. The alternative approach is to use questionnaire tests of student achievement or adult skills, such as the *Programme for International Student Assessment* (PISA) and the *International Adult Literacy Survey* (IALS) (see Figure 2.1). They measure only some aspects of skill and competence and are subject to survey and test limitations (for example, with respect to the size of sample, range of inter-related variables covered and coverage of countries).

Adding up individual embodiments of human capital is difficult...

Attempts have been made to aggregate data on projected labour market earnings of individuals by level of initial education over a lifetime[3] to arrive at an estimate of the value of human capital. Such an approach will omit the importance of "collective knowledge or skill" residing in organisations and other collective entities.[4] (In principle, individuals are unlikely to be able to extract a full rental from their organisation-specific skills in their wages, since their employer is the sole potential purchaser of those skills.) Aggregation is also likely to omit the impact of interactions and spillovers[5] arising from enhanced human capital in some members. Finally, the highly specific, culturally bound, non-communicative, tacit and heterogeneous dimensions of human capital are not easy to encapsulate in such aggregate measures of human capital.

... and the measurement of human capital needs to recognise the limitations of many proxies.

These caveats point to the need for considerable caution in estimations of stocks or flows of investment in human capital, especially at the international comparative level. Single-index measures of human capital need to be complemented with more specific measures based on direct measurement of knowledge and skills in organisations.

2.4. How is human capital developed?

Investment in skills takes place in many different settings and stages of the lifecycle...

Human capital formation takes place not only in formal education or training programmes, but also in informal interaction with others as well as through self-reflection and self-directed learning. The role of social networks and norms in fostering a culture of learning is important throughout the entire lifecycle. This section reviews empirical evidence on the impact of various factors on learning outcomes – evidence mainly available at primary and secondary levels of education – and draws on a very large literature covering various disciplines. Further details are provided in Appendices C and D.

Figure 2.1. **Comparative distribution of literacy levels**

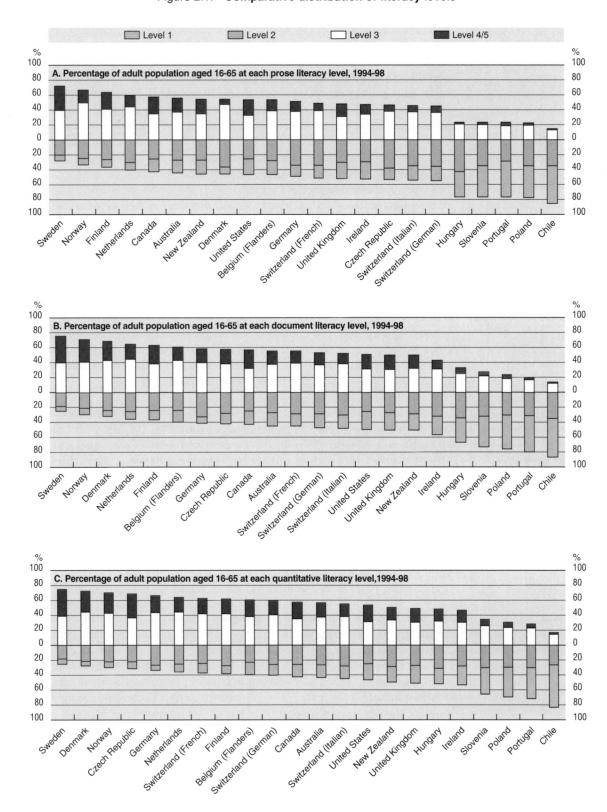

Note: Countries are ranked by the proportion in levels 3 and 4/5.
Source: OECD (2000), Literacy in the Information Age, Paris.

... and cultural context affects learning.

The importance of the cultural context in which learning and instruction take place has been emphasised by many. For example, Fuller and Clarke (1994) review a number of different approaches including what they describe as "policy mechanics"[6] and "classroom culturalist"[7] approaches to evaluating school productivity. As well as carrying particular norms and attitudes from their homes and social backgrounds, students learn particular norms, habits and values in the cultural setting of the school and classroom. These norms reinforce or modify perceptions of merit, status and norms of behaviour and participation as well as attitudes towards learning. Hence, the culturally constructed meanings attached to learning and instructional practices and tools may matter as much as the material content of school inputs or volume of resources expended. Fuller and Clarke claim that the culturalist approach, while it represents a valid perspective, has not been successful in producing empirical evidence on cross-cultural variability in meanings assigned to teaching tools and practices as well as identifying policy levers that can boost learning in different cultural settings.

Increased expenditure on education needs to be complemented by other strategies to enhance performance.

Public spending on education at all levels has been increasing in OECD countries over recent years, reflecting both increased participation (especially at the post-compulsory stages) as well as increased spending per student in real terms – often linked to reductions in school class sizes. The evidence suggests that spending does matter to learning outcomes but to a limited degree, and the efficacy of spending is very much tied to how teaching practices, school organisation and parental support combine with increased funding for education (Hanushek and Kim, 1995, Hanushek and Kimko, 2000 and Gundlach, Wossmann and Gmelin, 2000[8]).

There may be diminishing returns to spending on education for higher levels of economic development.

Some evidence suggests that there may be diminishing returns to spending on formal education in more economically developed countries (Hanushek and Kim, 1995). In developing countries, Fuller and Heyneman (1989) showed that school effects on achievement are greater than family background influences within impoverished settings, thus giving weight to public policy leverage in influencing student learning outcomes among the most disadvantaged. An important conclusion from much of the empirical work is that, in general, increased spending through expansion in educational participation (especially in achieving lower early school drop-out) may provide better returns (increased earnings in the labour market) than increased spending per student grade-year. This seems to hold for the United States (Betts and Roemer, 1998) as well as for developing countries (Psacharopolous, 1994).

Lower class sizes do appear to yield higher attainment, but the effect sizes are modest.

Much of the increased spending on education in recent decades has been devoted to reductions in class size. The question arises of whether future reductions in class size will be cost-effective. The effects depend on the age or needs group concerned – for example, smaller classes for young children (nursery schools or first grade year of elementary school) may have a positive impact. Research in the US and other OECD countries suggests that smaller classes do yield somewhat better attainment, according to student test data. However, whatever gains might be achieved as a result of smaller classes need to be weighed against the costs and the returns to alternative strategies such as attention to teacher training and quality. A large reduction in class size, say from 25 to 15 is likely to yield some improvement in results but the cost would be huge. It is likely that for specific subject areas, for specific groups of students and in combination with particular adaptations in teaching methods, smaller classes could yield improved results. Further research is needed on this possibility, linked to the policy option of using small class sizes for some purposes, and larger sizes for other purposes.

There is considerable agreement that family, social and home backgrounds bear on school effectiveness. Many studies point to the importance of factors such as the support, aspirations and work habits which parents provide their children. For example, Wossmann (2000), using data from a large number of countries participating in the *Third International Mathematics and Science Survey* (TIMSS), identifies parental influence over, and interest in, teaching of their children as well as curricular decisions as important influences over learning outcomes. Bourdieu (1979) uses the term "cultural capital" to describe the habits or cultural practices based on knowledge and demeanours learned through exposure to role models in the family and other environments. It also represents the collection of family-based resources such as parental education levels, social class, and family habits, norms and practices which influence academic success. Five major categories have been identified (Kellaghan *et al.*, 1993): work habits of the family, academic support and guidance, stimulation to explore and discuss ideas and events, language environment (opportunities for thinking and imagination) and academic aspirations and expectations.[9] Parents or siblings can help children with homework as well as in promoting values of learning and discipline. The higher the expectations of parents (particularly those of the mother), the lower is the probability of dropout. These can be effective buffers against the negative impact of low socio-economic status and low parental education attainment on children's academic outcomes (White and Kaufman, 1997).

The respective impact of families and schools is debated.

Coleman, who was primarily responsible for introducing the concept of social capital to educational research, emphasised the importance of a surrounding community of adults for young persons who are "embedded" in the enclaves of adults closest to them (Coleman, 1988). Social capital refers to the resources gained through social ties, memberships of networks and sharing of norms. By contrast, cultural capital – which is one dimension of social capital – refers to the resources residing in families whereby individuals attain a particular social status (Bourdieu, 1979; Bourdieu and Passeron, 1970). Families and students have access to varying amounts of financial, human, cultural and social capital, but such capital alone does not guarantee positive educational outcomes. Coleman argues learning can be supported by social capital through the existence of many types of supportive relations among adults who are parents of the children in the same school. The types of support relate to homework, out-of-school activities, and direct parental involvement in school activities and support for families and children in difficulty. Empirical evidence at US state level for the impact of social capital on student learning outcomes is shown by Putnam (2000a) (see Appendix C for details).

Social networks are important for learning.

Caution is needed in identifying the most significant determinants of student achievement. The mere presence of physical resources or highly trained teachers is not enough. Much depends on how the various actors including students, parents, teachers and those in the wider school community interact and make use of resources. The difficulty in identifying key factors is compounded by the susceptibility of results to what is being measured on the outcome side (impacts vary by subject area or skill domain) and to the population under examination (targeted support for particular groups may be more effective than for other groups). In general, stronger partnerships between students,

Partnerships, funding and effective regulatory arrangements matter.

parents, teachers supported by appropriate institutional and funding arrangements are vital.

Adult education needs to be carefully defined to be effective.

Demand for job-related training tends to be highest among young to mid-life workers and among those with higher than average levels of education. More generally, demand for continuing education and training is related to habits acquired and opportunities availed of earlier in life (OECD, 1998). Much adult learning is informal, experiential and inter-woven with daily living and working, making observation and measurement complex. It is difficult to observe and measure what makes for effective, high-quality informal learning. What evidence exists focuses more on formal or continuing education and training. Here, the evidence suggests that in the case of job-related training, programmes that meet the needs of individual learners and provide skills and knowledge related to the labour market are best developed in partnership with learners, providers and employers (OECD and US Department of Education, 1998). Formal, classroom or instruction-led settings may not guarantee effective learning outcomes since the context for learning is different and a greater range of customised treatments are called for. Moving to less formal and less job-related types of learning, a very wide range of experiences and settings are possible.[10] Identifying adult interests and not just adult skill deficiencies is important.

Social networks help to foster learning throughout life.

While different factors are difficult to disentangle, it does appear that high levels of social engagement and trust open up opportunities for learning, informal and formal. Ohsako (1998) quoting the results of the "International Comparison of Learning and Social Participation by the Elderly"[11](ICLSE) reports an association for senior citizens between the extent of participation in learning activities and active participation in community and social life. Voluntary associations can be important places for fostering a learning culture. There appears to be a strong inter-relationship between the level of initial education, continuing education and learning and levels of civic participation and trust pointing towards a virtuous circle. As will be noted in Chapter 3, some social networks may impede learning when, for example, the strength of familial or ethnic ties restricts opportunities for personal advancement and learning.[12]

2.5. How is human capital distributed?

Distribution is linked to overall standards and the quality of human capital.

Countries vary considerably with respect to the distribution of skills and learning opportunities for adults (OECD and Statistics Canada, 2000). Groups which are vulnerable to under-achievement, and therefore at risk of exclusion from the labour market and society, start out with a disadvantage at the beginning of formal education. Over time, this disadvantage may be compounded at school to bring about very poor patterns of graduation and progression to higher levels of education and into employment. Educational disadvantage has been defined and measured in various ways according to whether the focus is on individuals or groups, or whether the phenomena examined relate to funding, access, graduation or levels of achievement or skill proficiency in daily life. At the level of the school, one definition used has focused on the "child as being at a disadvantage at school if, because of economic, cultural or social factors, the competencies which the child brings to school differ from those valued in schools, and which are required to facilitate adaptation to school and school learning" (Kellaghan, 1999).

In most OECD countries the share of the adult population lacking basic numeracy and literacy skills has been declining, reflecting a lagged effect of the expansion of compulsory schooling in the latter half of the 20th century. Yet, it is not clear education has helped to narrow the gap between different social groups either in terms of access to further and higher education, or in terms of the relative position of different groups in the labour market and society. In some cases, expansion of demand for tertiary education may not have benefited those from socially disadvantaged backgrounds and may even have worsened the labour market position of the low-skilled. Supporting evidence for this is given in OECD (2001). Since the 1980s, income from employment has become more unequal in some OECD countries such as the USA, not only across, but also *within* different educational attainment groups. Possible explanations include greater variation in quality of initial education, changing demand for different types of skills not measured by initial education as well as other market or institutionally determined reasons (Levy and Murnane, 1999).

The position of the less advantaged has not improved in many countries...

A study by Blossfeld and Shavit (1993) of 13 countries[13] for two cohorts (born in 1910 and in 1960) showed that socio-economic background continued to have a strong determining effect on educational attainment and participation in most of the countries. This was especially true at the tertiary level where barriers (based on cost, information, motivation or prior ability) to wider participation persist in spite of expansion at the upper secondary level. They also found that the effects of social origin are stronger at lower transition stages (for example from lower to upper secondary education) with social selection occurring earlier on. Finally, the authors claimed that educational reform had little or no impact in terms of narrowing inequalities, with the possible exceptions of Sweden and the Netherlands. By contrast, Blossfeld and Shavit found evidence for some narrowing of gender differences alongside educational expansion.

... and despite policy initiatives in the area of educational equity, inequalities persist.

Erikson and Jonsson (1996) highlight three principal factors that underlie inequality in educational opportunities and outcomes across countries:

- Differences in "out-of-school" opportunities for learning.
- Differences in survival rates and opportunities for participation in "prestigious" educational tracks.
- Differences in global expansion of education.

Erikson and Jonsson draw attention to the role of the second of the above three factors in explaining differences among countries. Relative socio-economic equality together with comprehensive educational reform and lengthening of compulsory education helped diminish disparities over time. The older students are when they are able to leave school and called upon to choose between different educational tracks, the lower the risks of failure.

Although Hanushek and Somers (1999) find only weak evidence that public spending within and among US states is related to student achievement and ultimate labour market outcomes, other studies suggest that carefully designed and targeted programmes can have a positive impact on learning and life chances if they respond to the needs of individual learners from disadvantaged backgrounds (Kellaghan, 1999). For example, early childhood care

However, carefully designed and targeted programmes can have a positive impact.

and education can improve cognitive development during early childhood and result in long-term improvement in learning and school success (OECD, 1999a). Also, the impact of interventions aimed at disadvantaged youth cannot be assessed in terms of cognitive outcomes alone. Other possible benefits of socialisation and personal growth associated with such interventions should also be taken into account even though they are more difficult to measure.

Economic inequality goes hand in hand with inequality in educational access and adult literacy.

In the adult population, persons with low skills or levels of education are exposed to additional risks of unemployment and social exclusion (Steedman, 1996). Societies that tend to be less equal in terms of access to education and learning outcomes also tend to be less equal in terms of income distribution. Education, social background and access to social capital may act together to influence life chances. The OECD *International Adult Literacy Survey* (OECD and Statistics Canada, 2000) shows:

- Large differences in the overall level of literacy (comprising prose, document and quantitative literacy skills[14]) across countries.
- Large pockets of low skill, even in countries with high levels of educational attainment.
- A strong link between levels of literacy and outcomes in terms of labour market, civic participation and social outcomes.

Tackling disadvantage may be a key to raising overall standards.

Countries with a lower spread of literacy scores within the working-age population tend to perform better at the aggregate level on international comparisons. This suggests that a key to raising overall literacy standards and meeting future skill needs may be to address pockets of low skill linked to social and educational inequalities.

Willms (2001) shows a strong relationship between the family, educational and social background status of individuals on the one hand, and school achievement and adult literacy on the other. This holds for the different countries and for the different sub-groups within countries he analysed. This shows that for low levels of parental education or social status, there are wider variations in literacy performance within social sub-groups or countries than for higher levels.

Reinforcing the point, countries that have managed to reach high levels of adult literacy by international standards (notably the Nordic countries and the Czech Republic) appear to have done so in part by reducing the inequality between different social groups in terms of literacy. The United States is distinguished by high overall levels of educational attainment and medium-level scores on adult literacy, but is among those OECD countries showing the highest concentrations of low skill among the poorly educated. Hence, the potential impact of increasing literacy levels for the lowest levels appears to be high.

2.6. Changing demand for human capital

Mismatches between the demand and supply of human capital may be conceived in different ways.

Levels of *educational attainment* (specified by type or level), or *skills* in the labour force may be poorly matched with labour market demand. *"Qualifications inflation"* occurs when employers systematically upgrade the education requirements of jobs without a corresponding increase in skill content.

The rapid growth in educational attainment and levels of literacy in the past decade suggests that human capital is not in short supply in OECD countries. Many labour market analysts, including Hartog (1997), find evidence for what they call over-education both in Europe and the United States, with a possible increase over time in Europe. Green, McIntosh and Vignoles (1999) find evidence for some increase in over-education in the United Kingdom between the 1970s and 1980s but little evidence for widespread "qualifications inflation". However, the lack of any evidence of any widespread or long-term decline in estimated rates of return to education (OECD, 1998) cautions against an "over-education" hypothesis. Moreover, over-education is a somewhat loaded term, because it tends to ignore the wider functions of education, as an important resource used by people in their non-working lives, or as a source of well-being in itself.

Some evidence of "over-education" exists, particularly in respect of tertiary education...

Employers may be using educational qualifications as signals or "screening devices" to identify innate ability, motivation and aptitude, which are not necessarily the result of education (Spence, 1973). This means that the earnings associated with those qualifications may partly reflect those prior abilities, rather than the added value of the qualification. This process is termed "signalling". Few doubt that signalling plays some role in explaining educational wage differentials, but its overall importance remains controversial.[15]

Analysis of job and skill mismatches using data from the International Adult Literacy Survey (IALS) in the United Kingdom (Green, McIntosh and Vignoles, 1999) suggests that for any given level of education, not only lower levels of skill but under-utilisation of skills carries a penalty in terms of lower earnings in the labour market. Canadian university graduates with low levels of literacy skills were far more likely to experience job-education mismatch than other university graduates (Boothby, 1999).

... while at the same time evidence of under-skilling exists.

Structural changes in the economy, with growth in the high-technology sectors accompanied by rising educational requirements across all sectors, are changing the demand for skills. Levy and Murnane (1999) attribute US trends of increasing variation in wage income (within educational attainment groups) in part, to an increased premium for "soft skills" covering inter-personal communication, teamwork and problem-solving demanded by the growing personal services and marketing sectors. These "soft skills" are not reflected in completed educational levels – giving rise to differences in wage compensation within any given level of education. There is an emerging literature, which suggests that a growing wage gap in some countries could be explained by the differential returns to different types of skill (*e.g.* Carliner, 1996; Rivera-Batiz, 1994). These studies suggest that there may be a larger return to quantitative skills compared with prose reading skills in some countries, notably Canada, the United Kingdom and the United States.

More knowledge-intensive economies demand different skills...

Employers demand workers who are not only more skilled but also flexible and "trainable". Individual workers respond by upgrading on a strong platform of initial education and generic employability skills to achieve better employment openings. More intensive demand for "shared knowledge" and organisational capital at the level of organisations and firms implies a demand for not only more skilled individuals, but also for more effective management practices, team working and flexibility. The rise of new forms of organisational capital involving more teamwork, less hierarchical control and more individual

... and more flexibility and team-working skills to underpin new forms of organisational capital.

responsibility points towards new skills profiles and forms of inter-personal co-operation. Data from two British surveys conducted in 1986 and 1997 show increased demand for communications skills, "social skills" and problem-solving among recent company recruits (Green *et al.*, 1997). In more traditional and less knowledge-orientated sectors, there is a tendency for workers to be required to perform more narrowly defined tasks, although team working and flexibility are features of many traditional sector firms. These claims are supported elsewhere by studies of the workplace and firm organisations (for example, Cappelli and Rogovski, 1994; Freeman, Kleiner and Ostrogoff, 1997).

2.7. What is the impact of human capital on economic well-being?

Human capital has a positive impact on earnings, employment and economic growth.

One way of measuring the economic impact of human capital is through the calculation of productivity or earnings-based "rates of return" on investments in learning. Private rates of return can be estimated using data on private costs and post-tax earnings over a lifetime (see OECD, 1998). In principle such private rates of return should include the non-monetary benefits such as the pleasure of learning and the greater job satisfaction which may flow from a qualification. Social rates of return should combine the full range of public and societal costs and benefits involved in investing in more human capital. However, in practice, there are many difficulties in calculating the full costs and benefits, and published estimates often rest heavily on a relatively narrow range of measurable factors. In particular, it is difficult to take full account of the effects of in-work training on earnings, or the benefits of human capital which accrue to society generally, or of the many non-economic benefits. An alternative approach is to seek empirical evidence, using national or regional data, of the impact of the stock and rate of change of human capital on the levels and rates of economic growth. There is a large literature which seeks to make such estimates, using both micro and macro-economic data.

2.7.1. The micro-level evidence on earnings and employment

Education is positively correlated with employment and earnings.

Better-educated people are more likely to be in work, and if economically active, less likely to be unemployed. Better qualifications also attract wage premia. In some countries, these are very large, reflecting a greater wage spread in the labour market and possibly higher returns to particular skills. Micro-economic evidence indicates that an additional year of education is associated with, on average, between 5 and 15% higher earnings (Krueger and Lindahl, 1999).

Independently of qualifications, adult literacy has a strong impact on earnings.

A related area of research examines the impact on earnings of different types of adult literacy. Evidence from the US suggests that economic returns to literacy skill increase with the knowledge intensity of jobs (Raudenbush and Kasim, 1998). In a British longitudinal survey, Bynner *et al.* (2001) reported returns on earnings of 8-10% for Level 1 numeracy according to the UK Qualification and Curriculum Authority (QCA).[16] Data from the International Adult Literacy Survey (OECD and Statistics Canada, 2000) show that education, literacy, experience, gender, parents' education and use of native language – all of which are related to human capital – account for between 20 and 50 per cent of total variation in labour market earnings (figure 4.10, p. 76). The linkage between literacy skills and educational attainment on the one hand, and earnings on the other, varies between countries. This implies varying national and institutional effects on the way in which literacy skills are rewarded by national labour markets.

2.7.2. The macro-level evidence on growth in GDP

A standard model of economic growth based on physical capital and labour was developed by Solow (1956). In this model, output grows faster than the two main economic inputs – capital and labour – leaving a "residual" factor representing technical progress. Critics of such "growth accounting" exercises point out that measuring the quality of the stock of human capital is problematic. Moreover, as Barro and Sala-I-Martin (1995) observe, use of growth accounting does not provide any guide to the relevant counterfactual evidence.[17]

An alternative approach to measuring the impact of various factors on growth in GDP is to use cross-country regressions incorporating variables for physical capital, education, level of income and in some cases proxy variables for various social and institutional factors (Barro, 2001). However, the selection of countries, variables included, choice of time periods and the specification of models[18] can make a substantial difference to the results obtained. Some studies include both developing and developed countries in the analysis. This increases the power of the statistical tests employed because of the greater variation in the posited determinants of growth. However it also implicitly assumes common determinants of growth in developing and developed countries – although they are quantitatively different across both.

In the early models of economic growth, there was no explicit role for different levels and quality of education and no account of the potential of human capital to generate "externalities" or "spillover" effects (through, for example, its impact on the productivity of other factors). With the development of so-called "new growth" models (Lucas, 1988; Romer, 1990b; Barro and Sala-i-Martin, 1995), the role of education and learning in generating new technology and innovation received more emphasis. New designs and ideas created by research and development and knowledge-intensive sectors enhance the productivity of physical capital investment in other sectors and regions. Internally generated technical change, increasing returns to scale, the know-how acquired in the course of technology-intensive production can fuel growth in output. For example, a growing, "leading-edge" export sector can leverage knowledge and innovation throughout the whole economy through mobility of skills and entrepreneurs and dissemination of new technologies and products. The initial stock of human capital in a previous period can generate innovation and downstream effects in the form of "spillovers" or positive "externalities" which affect other firms and even regions or countries (Acemoglu, 1996). Part of this initial stock refers to basic or applied scientific knowledge acquired in higher education. Harberger (1998) distinguishes between "yeast" and "mushroom" effects on the residual in economic growth models. Knowledge and human capital act like yeast to increase productivity relatively evenly across the economy, while other factors such as a technological breakthrough or discovery suddenly mushroom to increase productivity more dramatically in some sectors than others.

Higher education is important for the development of innovative research and the ability to acquire and adopt it. Hence, some "new growth" theories have tried to build a more complex model, accounting for human capital formation by giving prime importance not just to education itself, but also to its by-products such as research and innovation. When, for instance, spending on research and development is included in growth models, the

There are many difficulties in accounting for the role of human capital in growth.

Knowledge spillovers are of key importance...

... particularly in the link between higher education and applied research and development.

29

independent effect of schooling appears to be reduced. Using R&D spending relative to GDP as an approximation for technological know-how, Nonneman and Vanhoudt (1996) find that some of the attribution of growth to initial education was instead associated with R&D spending.

Ambiguity in previous research findings on education and growth may be linked to poor data quality.

Studies of the impact of education on economic growth have often been inconclusive. This may partly be linked to poor data quality and partly to the difficulty of identifying the complex interactions through which human capital plays a role in the growth process. Pritchett (1999) claims that increases in educational enrolment or attainment had no significant positive impact on the rate of growth of productivity or economic growth.[19] Examples of proxy measures typically used for human capital include: gross enrolment rates (*e.g.* percentage enrolled in secondary education); average years of completed education in the adult population; estimates of the proportion of the labour force or adult population which has received primary, secondary or tertiary education; or estimates of educational quality where the results of student test scores or adult literacy surveys are employed. In analysing the impact of these proxy variables on economic growth, there are a number of measurement pitfalls and analytical challenges which are difficult to overcome.

i) The direction of causation is sometimes not clear.

ii) The role of human capital may be obscured by its interaction with other factors: adaptation of new technologies and work organisation and more effective allocations of physical capital.

iii) Completed level of education is a crude proxy for the role of knowledge and skills.

iv) Measurement error due to an inappropriate or non-comparable classification of educational completion according to international standards.

v) Atypical or "outlier" countries may bias results (Temple, 2001).

An example of *ii)* above occurs when models fail to reflect the way in which some countries with low initial stocks of human capital at the beginning of the 1960s may have had greater opportunities and incentives to grow by importing and implementing technology developed abroad. Alternatively, countries with low initial levels of income but high initial stocks of human capital (or a critical mass of higher education graduates) may benefit from a catch-up or convergence process by adopting or applying imported technologies.

An example of *iv)* above is given by Steedman (1996) who points to inconsistencies in the way data on attainment were reported and classified under the *International Standard Classification of Education* (ISCED). Krueger and Lindahl (1999) also believe that measurement error in the main international data sources used may be at the source of these results, especially in relation to the negative results for attainment of females.[20] The latter result is difficult to reconcile with the view that education of girls and women does make an important contribution to economic growth and welfare in both developed and developing countries.[21]

Measures of human capital based on direct measures of skills show more positive results...

One drawback of most cross-country work is the likelihood of important differences in the nature and quality of schooling across countries, which could undermine the usefulness of international comparisons (Temple, 2001). Hanushek and Kimko (2000) and Barro (2001), using data on international tests of cognitive ability in mathematics and science, estimate the quality of different groups in the adult labour force. They found that using measures based on the quality of education provides a more powerful explanation of economic growth in different countries than simply years of schooling.

More recent work by de la Fuente and Domenech (2000) and Bassanini and Scarpetta (2001) has strengthened the case for seeing measurement error as an important part of the story. De la Fuente and Domenech (2000) examined the Barro-Lee data set[22] and other data sources such as that of Nehru, Swanson and Dubey (1995). Examining the intertemporal consistency of this data set and comparing the data with more recent data from the OECD education indicators database, they found considerable measurement problems. They then proceeded to construct an improved data set using available national and international sources, with an eye to ensuring coherence over time as well as agreement with recently collected OECD data on educational attainment. Using this data set, they find that human capital *does* have a substantial and positive impact on growth in GDP or income per capita. The results are noteworthy in that they relate to a limited sample of countries (mainly OECD members) whereas in most of the other studies, significant results were obtained with a mixture of high and low-income countries. When confined to OECD countries, analyses from many studies had frequently shown no significant impact of human capital on growth (*e.g.* Barro, 2001).

... and recent empirical work has produced more robust estimates of the impact of human capital on economic growth.

Further work by the OECD on recent divergences in rates of economic growth has made use of the data developed by de la Fuente and Domenech. This OECD work shows that "the improvement in human capital has been one of the key factors behind the growth process of the past decades in all OECD countries, but especially so in Germany (mainly in the 1980s), Italy, Greece, the Netherlands (mainly in the 1980s) and Spain where the increase in human capital accounted for more than half a percentage point acceleration in growth with respect to the previous decade" (OECD, 2000*b*). For OECD countries as a whole, the implication is that each extra year of full-time education (corresponding to a rise in human capital by about 10 per cent), is associated with an increase in output per capita of about 6 per cent. (This estimate is based on the preferred specification. Alternative specifications suggest a range of 4-7%.)

Since universal participation has been achieved in most OECD countries up to the end of compulsory or even upper secondary education, there is a particular interest in the growth-inducing role of higher or post-compulsory education. The evidence is not well developed since suitable time-series data are not generally available. However, a study by Gemmell (1996) using an index of labour force education – numbers of workers who have passed through primary, secondary and tertiary education – investigates the effects of the three levels of education across developing and OECD countries over the 1960-85 period. Splitting the country samples by income level, he finds that, other things equal, tertiary education seems to be more important for economic growth in OECD countries, while primary and secondary education are more important for economic growth in developing countries. Using enrolment data, Gemmell (1995), obtained similar results, whereas Barro and Sala-I-Martin (1995) found similar results using eductional attainment.[23] Both the initial level and subsequent growth of tertiary education were found to be positively and significantly associated with per capita income growth in OECD countries.

Higher education is particularly important in OECD countries.

The potential for higher education to generate significant productivity spillover effects may account for the difference in results obtained from micro and macro-level studies of income. In the former case, estimates of private returns to higher education appear to be modest in comparison with upper secondary education (OECD, 1998). However, at the macro-economic level, the role of higher education in generating indirect and spillover effects may be better captured, thus resulting in more significant impacts.

Field of study at higher education is also relevant.

Two further considerations in assessing the impacts of higher education on productivity may be the balance between different fields of study and the extent to which higher education graduates enter sectors of the economy whose contribution to GDP is not well measured (such as for example public administration or services). Investigating the impact of human capital on labour productivity growth for OECD countries during 1950-88, Gittleman and Wolff (1995) found that the number of scientists and engineers per capita has a significant positive impact on productivity.

Human capital is a factor in income equality.

Human capital also affects patterns of income inequality. Income inequality, which has tended to increase in many OECD countries since the mid-1980s, has been related to many factors. Increased inequality between households according to type of employment (part-time, temporary, etc.) has been associated with increases in work-rich and work-poor shares of households (OECD and Statistics Canada, 2000). Alesina and Rodrik (1992) show a link between education and the distribution of income with causality running in both directions. Data from the International Adult Literacy Survey (OECD and Statistics Canada, 2000) indicate a high correlation between country levels of income inequality and inequality in the distribution of literacy (prose), suggesting that more evenly spread levels of human capital are associated with greater income equality.

In summary, recent research suggests a favourable impact of human capital on economic growth.

A generally favourable picture of the impact of human capital has emerged from a review by Temple (2001) in which he concludes:

"Over the last ten years, growth researchers have bounced from identifying quite dramatic effects of education, to calling into question the existence of any effect at all. More recent research is placed somewhere between these two extremes, but perhaps leaning closer to the original findings that education has a major impact. In examining the studies that have not detected an effect, we have some convincing reasons (measurement error, outliers, and incorrect specification) to doubt such results. The balance of recent evidence points to productivity effects of education which are at least as large as those identified by labour economists."

2.8. What is the impact of human capital on all aspects of human well-being?

A number of methodologies have been developed to measure the "social benefits" of education and learning and these are described below. The evidence reviewed in this section bears mainly on the measured impacts of initial education in areas such as health, social insurance, parenting, crime and personal or subjective well-being. Some of the influences of learning on health and social behaviour may be mediated by the fostering of habits, characteristics and attitudes which assist job creation, productivity, personal well-being, positive time preferences and self-discipline. Some of these characteristics as well as innate abilities and attributes are formed outside formal education but are highly correlated with schooling.

Human competence can be put to socially destructive purposes such as crime. Pursuit of some forms of human capital may also preclude other desirable goals and may undermine social relationships and personal well-being. For example, an excessive focus on cognitive skills in the early years of childhood at the expense of socialisation and play may not be best attuned to the development needs of children. As with social capital, these potential negative impacts are the exception.

Positive social impacts of education outweigh negative impacts...

A number of important measurement techniques have been developed to place a monetary value on particular social benefits of education, including health. Work by Wolfe and Haveman (2001), McMahon (2001)[24] and Wolfe and Zuvekas (1997) provides a range of estimation techniques offering monetary estimates of the social benefits flowing from education. These rely on calculations of the cost of "purchasing" the same effects by alternative means.[25] Behrman and Stacey (1997) summarise work on a variety of sources of wider social impacts, drawing mainly on evidence from the United States. Other evidence on the wider social benefits of education has emerged in recent reports in the United Kingdom.[26]

... and the indirect impact of education on economic growth via social benefits may be as large as the direct impacts.

Using controls for income, race, social status and other variables, research has shown that education tends to be correlated with better health, lower crime, political and community participation and social cohesion. However, care needs to be taken in interpreting these results, since the direction of causation is unclear, and other uncontrolled factors may be at work. However, the conclusion of Wolfe and Haveman (2001) as well as McMahon (2001) is that the social benefits of education are large – possibly larger than the direct labour market and macro-economic effects.

One of the clearest benefits of education is better health. Individuals with higher educational attainment have healthier habits and lifestyles. More educated individuals are less likely to smoke or to drink heavily. An additional year of schooling has been estimated to reduce average daily cigarette consumption by 1.6 for men and 1.1 for women (Wolfe and Haveman, 2001). Better-educated people are also less likely to be overweight and tend to engage in more exercise per week than are less educated people – about 17 minutes for each additional year of schooling (Kenkel, 1991). The associated health benefits of education may be due, in part, to occupational choices (choosing occupations with relatively lower occupational hazards) or locational choices (electing to live in less polluted areas). More highly educated individuals are likely to be better skilled at identifying relevant health-related information and in using this information to achieve behaviour conducive to better health (Kenkel, 1991). However, Kenkel demonstrates using US data that most of the variation in health outcomes cannot be explained by differences in knowledge relating to health. Education appears to have an effect on health independent of income, race, social background and other factors.

Better educated people tend to be healthier...

Higher levels of education are associated with a lower probability of receiving social transfer benefits (Wolfe and Haveman, 2001). Recent analyses have found that higher education of mothers reduces the probability that their daughters will, if eligible for welfare benefits, elect to receive them. Studies of applicants for disability transfers also find that more education decreases the probability of receiving disability-related transfers. More edu-

... have a lower take-up of social benefits...

cated workers also tend to have lower unemployment rates and receive higher wages, by which society benefits from more taxes.[27]

... and pass on some of the education benefits to their children.

Educational attainment in one generation has positive effects on the educational attainment of the next generation. Children of parents with upper secondary attainment are themselves more likely to complete upper secondary than are children of less well educated parents (Sandefur, McLanahan and Wojtkiewicz, 1989). Better-schooled parents have children with a higher level of cognitive development as well as children with higher future earnings potential. There is also evidence of community-level spillovers in so far as living in higher education level communities increases the probability that the children living in the community will complete secondary schooling, other things constant (Wolfe and Haveman, 2001).

Education improves labour market search and produces more efficient consumers...

Education has a positive influence on labour market search, plausibly because of skills in using information as well as the capacity to use networks to access information and make important connections. More educated individuals also appear to be more efficient consumers (Rizzo and Zeckhauser, 1992).

... and is linked to civic participation.

The level of completed education is one of the most important predictors of many forms of political and social engagement. Verba, Schlozman and Brady (1995) found that education, other things constant, increases political participation. Moreover, literacy skills among adults have shown a positive relationship with participation in voluntary community activities for several OECD countries (OECD and Statistics Canada, 2000). Bynner *et al.* (2001) using data for the United Kingdom report higher levels of "social skills" for higher levels of education. These cover organising, advising and counselling skills – all of which have the potential to enhance the quality of civic engagement. They also reports higher tolerance of diversity, commitment to equality of opportunities and resistance to political alienation.

Some of the findings are more ambiguous. Helliwell and Putnam (1999*b*) found that increases in average education levels increased levels of trust and did not reduce political participation levels, while Nie, Junn and Stehlik-Barry (1996) argue that *relative* rather than *absolute* levels of education are the key determinant of civic participation.

Education is also correlated with lower crime...

Education lowers the risk of crime through helping to socialise young people who remain in school. Wolfe and Haveman (2001) find a positive effect of neighbourhood human capital variables on anti-social behaviour. Although the total impact of these social benefits take time to appear, society may benefit from investing in education by paying less for social welfare programmes and crime prevention/law enforcement.

... and with volunteering and giving.

There is also evidence that the amount of time and money devoted to charity is positively associated with the amount of schooling. For example, one study found that college graduates volunteered nearly twice as many hours and donated 50% more of their income than high school graduates (Hodgkinson and Weitzman, 1988). In the United Kingdom, the National Child Development Study (NCDS) data reveals a strong correlation between levels of education and membership of political organisations, environment or women's groups and charity, residents and parent-teacher associations, (Schuller *et al.*, 2001). Bynner *et al.* (2001) report that UK higher education graduates are three times more likely to be a current or active member of a voluntary organisation than those without upper secondary completion (below A-Levels) and about twice as likely as upper secondary completers.

Evidence suggests that education has both immediate and long-term positive effects on self-reported happiness. Blanchflower and Oswald (2000) report estimates of "happiness equations", in regressions that relate self-reported well-being to various individual characteristics. They find that educational attainment is associated with greater happiness, even when controlling for family income. It is possible that the extent of an individual's education has a positive effect on the happiness of others, in which case self-interested individuals may tend to under-invest in education from a social point of view. Alternatively, education may affect happiness because it influences perceptions of status relative to others, in which case the results of Blanchflower and Oswald could overstate the effect on well-being of an expansion of educational provision. However, Putnam (2001) finds that, using state-level data from the United States, both one's own level of education, and average county level of education have positive effects on happiness.

There is a growing literature on the relationship between education and subjective well-being and happiness.

2.9. Summing up

Education, training and learning can play important roles in providing the basis for economic growth, social cohesion and personal development. Investment in human capital takes time to develop and yield benefits. In so far as impacts can be measured and compared, some studies suggest that the social impacts of learning (health, crime, social cohesion) could be as large as the impacts on economic productivity, if not larger. However, a correlation between aggregate indicators of schooling and various economic and social outcomes provides no indication of the right direction for formal education, apart from the observation that more learning is beneficial. There are synergies and complementarities between learning and other dimensions of the social, institutional and legal environments. Skills and competencies can have an indirect influence through enhancing the impact of other factors. Higher education in partnership with public and private interests can play a key role in stimulating research and innovation conducive to faster growth in national income.

There are significant pay-offs to additional learning...

This chapter identified a potentially strong interaction between human and social capital. Learning and preparation for learning that is nurtured within families and local communities provides an important basis for continuing acquisition of human capital through formal education and learning throughout adult life. Social networks and learning organisations can also stimulate informal learning "on-the-job" and in daily life. However, the links between human and social capital are not automatic.

An increase in aggregate human capital also needs to be complemented with strategies which attend to:

1. the quality of investment in human capital and the relevance of skills to social and economic demands;

2. the distribution of learning opportunities within countries given the links between inequality and overall performance; and

... and the quality and distribution of learning opportunities are important.

3. the potential for market "under-investment" because of the "public good" or "externalities" characteristics of human capital.

Human capital measures need to look at actual skills, as well as inputs like time spent in education.

Finally, given the growing policy consensus on the importance of lifelong and lifewide learning, (the latter implying a range of learning environments) there is an emerging awareness of the problems of focusing unduly on narrow interpretations and measures of human capital. Outcome-based measures, such as surveys of literacy and numeracy skills, are clearly a very important way of directly measuring human capital. Given the complementary strengths and weaknesses of traditional input based measures of human capital and direct survey-based measures, any comprehensive measurement strategy will need to use both approaches.

Notes

1. Inglehart (1997) defines culture as a "system of attitudes, values and knowledge that is widely shared within a society and is transmitted from generation to generation" (p. 15). Culture is learned and changes relatively slowly. Inglehart argues that culture is more likely to change through replacement of older generations by younger generations than through shifts in values and attitudes of individuals who have assimilated core beliefs and values from early childhood onwards.

2. Human capital shares common features with physical capital to the extent that it involves *i*) a time dimension where investments take place and benefits accrue, and *ii*) forgoing short-term benefit. However, it differs from physical capital to the extent that the normal rules of alienability and consumer sovereignty whereby consumers can purchase and "own" an external good do not apply. By definition, human capital is embodied in individuals and its services can be sold on the market but, strictly speaking, its ownership cannot be transferred or sold except in conditions of human slavery.

3. The value of human capital stock can be estimated by the present value of a future stream of net additions to earnings flowing from acquiring additional education and training less the costs of investing in this additional education and training over a lifecycle, discounted by some social rate of return to reflect the opportunity cost of investing in more education.

4. Although human capital is defined as a property or characteristic of individuals, the aggregation and combination of different quantities of individual human capital leads to organisation-level competence which has impacts over and above those of the individual parts.

5. Spillovers occur when increased skills of some contribute to higher productivity not only for those with skills but others as well who benefit from the higher productivity of the highly-skilled.

6. The "policy mechanics" approach seeks to identify discrete school inputs which make a significant difference to school and learning outcomes.

7. According to the "classroom culturalist" approach, the role of norms and socialisation in the classroom is important for an understanding of achievement and school effectiveness.

8. Gundlach, Wossmann and Gmelin (2000) use international test data on student achievement in mathematics and science over the period 1970 to 1994 to claim that school productivity has, at best, not increased in nine out of eleven OECD countries studied in spite of increased spending per student.

9. There have been a few recent attempts at identifying proxies for cultural capital. So far, they have focused on outside activities by families (*e.g.* attending a symphony concert, visiting an art gallery, travelling), weekly occurrences of activities in the home (*e.g.* family discussions, evening meal, debates about issues outside the home), the types of reading materials available in the home (*e.g.* daily newspaper, encyclopædia, books of poetry), as well as languages understood and spoken by the mother or father (see Willms, 1999).

10. Examples of innovative practices in locating learning opportunities and facilities close to where people work, live and travel are reviewed in the publication "How Adults Learn" (OECD and US Department of Education, 1998).

11. The countries included were: Germany, Korea, Japan, Sweden, the United Kingdom and the United States.

12. Field and Spence (2000) in their study of adult learning in Northern Ireland find that, whereas dense social ties organised on family and religious community lines are associated with high achievement in initial education, these ties may impede participation in formal, continuing adult education. Part of the reason for this may be a substitution of dense family and local community ties for participation in formal continuing education or training. A lack of social capital which bridges across different communities may provide little incentive for individuals and local groups to participate in more formal or structured types of education and learning. However, strong intra-community social capital ties (analogous to "bonding social capital" discussed in Chapter 3 below) may foster higher levels of informal adult learning because adults rely on family and community networks for information and social engagement.

13. Czechoslovakia, England and Wales, Federal Republic of Germany, Hungary, Israel, Italy, Japan, the Netherlands, Poland, Sweden, Switzerland, Taiwan and the United States.

14. IALS was conducted amongst persons aged 16-65 to test the capacity of adults to use printed and written information. Prose literacy covered capacity to read and understand continuous text; document literacy related to the ability to interpret reports, documents and various types of "discontinuous text"; while quantitative literacy related to ability to interpret quantitative information such as mathematical charts and displays usually embedded in prose. Literacy was measured not as a dichotomy of literate versus illiterate, but according to a measurable skill continuum.

15. Weiss (1995), among others, provides very different perspectives on the theoretical generality and empirical validity of signalling models.

16. Bynner *et al.* (2001) also found that improvement in basic skills to reach national adult literacy targets in 2010 could lead to a saving of £2.5 billion to the taxpayers for numeracy improvements and £0.4 billion for reading literacy improvements.

17. Temple (2001) remarks "As an example, consider a claim that X percentage points of growth in a given country is due to a change in the quality of the labour force. This does not imply that, in the absence of the change in labour force quality, the growth rate of output would have been precisely X percentage points lower. The problem is that educational attainment may have other, indirect effects on output through labour force participation, investment, and even R&D and the growth of total factor productivity. Growth accounting does not capture these indirect effects, and so it is necessarily silent on the overall importance to growth of variables like education".

18. For example, the relation between years of schooling and output is affected by whether levels, rates of change or semi-logarithmic forms are used. It cannot be assumed that returns to education are independent of the initial level.

19. Pritchett also uses the growth rate of total factor productivity in a growth accounting framework to arrive at essentially the same conclusion.

20. Barro and Sala-i-Martin (1995) and Barro and Lee (1997) find that initial levels of female education (both secondary and tertiary) appear to be inversely related to growth.

21. Other studies indicate a strong correlation between a mothers' level of education and the lifetime health of her children.

22. The well-known Barro-Lee data set gives a historical series of educational attainment data for the population 25+. The data set was compiled largely from census results collected by the UN Statistics Division with estimates for missing years.

23. For a large sample of countries they found that higher education had large effects – increasing average male secondary schooling by 0.68 years raised annual growth by 1.1 percentage points per year while an increase of 0.09 years in average tertiary education raises annual growth by 0.5 percentage points.

24. Using data for 78 countries, McMahon examines interactions among various social outcomes such as health, democratisation, reduction of inequality in the income distribution and poverty, environmental impacts, and crime. He finds that more than half of the total effects of education are due to induced indirect effects such as improved health which feed back on growth in income per capita.

25. Hence, it is possible to use information on revealed preferences of individuals in purchasing a given level of health through private expenditure in order to compute the monetary value of more education by adding up the values of increments in various social outcomes including lower crime, better health, etc.

26. Bynner *et al.* (2001), Bynner and Egerton (forthcoming) and Schuller *et al.* (2001).

27. This result follows from the facts that more educated workers tend to work more continuously on average and the taxes taken from these workers are proportionally higher as they are taxed at higher marginal rates due to higher salaries.

Chapter 3

THE EVIDENCE ON SOCIAL CAPITAL

"Virtually every commercial transaction has within itself an element of trust, certainly any transaction conducted over a period of time. It can be plausibly argued that much of the economic backwardness in the world can be explained by a lack of mutual confidence." Kenneth J. Arrow, "Gifts and Exchanges", *Philosophy and Public Affairs*, 1, Summer 1972, p. 357.

3.1. Introduction

Societies founded on networks of trust and co-operation can help to realise human potential. There is a growing awareness in the economic literature of the importance of social networks and trust in supporting collective endeavours. For example Temple (2001) observed in relation to social capital that "It provides a useful umbrella term for those aspects of societies which, though difficult to measure and incorporate into formal models, are widely thought to be an important determinant of long-run economic success. For some economists (not all) the intuition that 'society matters' is strong enough to outweigh the current absence of much in the way of a theoretical underpinning".

Alongside individual skills, social relationships are important to human achievement.

This chapter considers the definition, measurement and impacts of social capital. Since the term is relatively new and its meaning is not universally agreed, this chapter maps out one possible approach to the definition of the concept and measurement of its contributions to well-being. Although the evidence is, as yet, tentative, it does suggest that the concept of social capital is a useful one for policy purposes, and that further work is needed to develop the concept and establish measurement techniques.

3.2. Different concepts of social capital

The concept of "social capital" is different from human and physical capital in a number of respects since it:

Social capital resides in social relationships, and as capital, may be conceived as a resource in which we invest to provide a stream of benefits.

- is relational rather than being the exclusive property of any one individual;

- is mainly a public good in that it is shared by a group; and

- is produced by societal investments of time and effort, but in a less direct fashion than is human or physical capital.

Social capital is also the product of inherited culture and norms of behaviour. Hence, social capital has "social" and "capital" dimensions since it resides in relations rather than individuals being also a resource that can generate a steam of benefits for society over time. However, it can also lead to dysfunction when used by one group against others.

Social capital depends on the actions of the individuals who support it.

Many users of the term "social capital" have applied an individualistic approach to understanding the incentives of individuals to use social capital and invest in its acquisition (Glaeser, 2001). To some extent, Coleman emphasised the instrumental nature of social capital in achieving certain outcomes. Others, including Hirschman, have emphasised the efforts of individuals to act collectively to achieve non-monetary goals such as justice, beauty, love, community, and friendship. This non-instrumental aspect of collective action represents "an investment in individual and group identity" (Hirschman, 1984). Hirschman focuses on the value of "social energy" in the form of friendship, shared ideals and ideas that transcend rational self-interest and market transactions and promote social co-operation. Whatever the motivation for co-operating and trusting, investment in individual and group identity can lead to the creation of dense social networks and ultimately better economic and social outcomes. In this way, civic engagement, honesty and social trust can reinforce each other.

The roots of the concept lie in earlier research.

The idea of social capital can be traced to the work of Alexis de Tocqueville,[1] Emile Durkheim[2] and Max Weber[3] (for an extensive account of the historical roots of the concept see Woolcock, 1998). The first known reference to "social capital" in its contemporary sense was in the context of its importance for education and local communities (Hanifan, 1916). Since then, social capital has been used by Jacobs (1961)[4] in her analysis of city neighbourhoods, by Loury (1987) in a study of labour markets, by Coleman (1988) who stressed its complementarity with human capital and by Putnam (1993) and Fukuyama (1995) who applied the concept at the level of nation state or region (the former emphasising the role of civic engagement in fostering democracy and social cohesion). Bourdieu (1979) and Bourdieu and Passeron (1970) used a closely related concept, "cultural capital" (see Section 2.4, Chapter 2).

There are four main approaches to the definition of social capital.

There is no single definition of social capital. At least four broad approaches to the concept may be distinguished:

1. The anthropological literature is the source for the notion that humans have natural instincts for association. For example, Fukuyama (1999) stresses the biological basis for social order and the roots of social capital in human nature.

2. The sociological literature describes social norms and the sources of human motivation. It emphasises features of social organisation such as trust, norms of reciprocity and networks of civic engagement.

3. The economic literature draws on the assumption that people will maximise their personal utility, deciding to interact with others and draw on social capital resources to conduct various types of group activities (Glaeser, 2001). In this approach, the focus is on the investment strategies of individuals faced with alternative uses of time.

4. A strand in the political science literature emphasises the role of institutions, political and social norms in shaping human behaviour. Recent work at the World Bank on the role of social capital in reducing poverty and promoting sustainable development has emphasised the role of institutions, social arrangements, trust and networks.[5]

One approach has linked the concept of social capital to broader macro-institutional issues or what some economists refer to as "social capabilities" (*e.g.* Abramovitz and David, 1996; Omori, 2001; Hall and Jones, 1999; Temple and Johnson, 1998.) However, Putnam (2001a), Woolcock (2001) and Knack (1999) prefer a "lean and mean" definition that focuses on social networks and the immediately linked norms of reciprocity (or trust in the case of Knack). Some commentators (e.g. Woolcock, 2001) see trust as an outcome of social capital (defined as networks and associated norms), while others view trust as a component of shared values and norms which constitute social capital.

In this report, the definition of social capital is: *networks together with shared norms, values and understandings that facilitate co-operation within or among groups*. Networks relate to the objective behaviour of actors who enter into associative activity. Shared norms, values and understandings relate to the subjective dispositions and attitudes of individuals and groups, as well as sanctions and rules governing behaviour, which are widely shared.[6] The cultural context in which shared attitudes, values and knowledge are transmitted from generation to generation is important in understanding the choices of individuals and groups in relation to co-operation. Shared norms and values enable people to communicate and make sense of common experiences as well as divergences in some norms and values. Different systems of values and meanings can exist alongside shared ones without necessarily undermining co-operation, if a climate of tolerance prevails. Hence, dialogue and mutual understanding founded on tolerance of different cultures or beliefs, are important dimensions of social cohesion and help to underpin social capital.

This report offers its own definition.

Trust may be viewed as both a source and an outcome of social capital as well as being a very close proxy for many of the norms, understandings and values which underpin social co-operation. A distinction can be drawn between: whether people *trust* others; and whether people are *trustworthy*. Trust may be a good proxy for trustworthiness (allowing for time lags), but trustworthiness describes behaviour which results from a multitude of factors including networks and shared values and norms. Three types of trust need to be distinguished:

Trust supports social capital.

- inter-personal trust among familiars (family, close work colleagues and neighbours);
- inter-personal trust among "strangers"; and
- trust in public and private institutions.

Social capital allows individuals, groups and communities to resolve collective problems more easily. Norms of reciprocity and networks help ensure compliance with collectively desirable behaviour. In the absence of trust and networks ensuring compliance, individuals tend not to co-operate because others cannot be relied on to act in a similar way. Social capital may be a by-product of various social activities not necessarily undertaken with a view to strengthening social capital.[7] As with the case of human capital, social capital has "positive externalities" such that many people benefit from the contributions of one individual or group to social capital. It therefore risks underinvestment because the contributing actors do not fully appropriate its benefits. As Coleman observed: "The result is that there will be in society an imbalance between the relative investment in organisations that produce private goods for a market and in organisations (often voluntary associations) from which the benefits are not captured" (Coleman, 1990, p. 317). However, access to information and influence through social networks also confers pri-

Social capital is partly a public and partly a private good.

vate benefits on individuals and in some cases can be used by individuals or groups to exclude others and reinforce dominance or privilege.

Bonding, bridging and linking are important dimensions of social capital.

Three basic forms of social capital have been identified: social bonds, bridges and linkages (Woolcock, 1999). Bonding refers typically to relations among members of families and ethnic groups. Bridging social capital refers to relations with distant friends, associates and colleagues. Linking refers to relations between different social strata in a hierarchy where power, social status and wealth are accessed by different groups. Woolcock (2001) relates linking social capital to the capacity of individuals and communities to leverage resources, ideas, and information from formal institutions beyond the immediate community radius.

Both bonding and bridging social capital are needed to avoid social fragmentation.

Although strong bonding ties give particular communities or groups a sense of identity and common purpose, without "bridging" ties that transcend various social divides (*e.g.* religion, ethnicity, socio-economic status), bonding ties can become a basis for the pursuit of narrow interests, and can actively exclude outsiders. Relatively homogeneous groups may be characterised by strong trust and co-operative norms within a group, but low trust and co-operation with the rest of society. Some forms of exclusive bonding can then be a barrier to social cohesion and personal development. These are examples of weak bridging but strong bonding. As Powell and Smith-Doerr (1994) observed: "the ties that bind may also turn into ties that blind."

Closely-knit groups may exclude outsiders.

A restricted radius of trust within a tightly knit group, such as family members or closed circles of friends, can promote forms of social interaction that are inward-seeking and less orientated to trust and co-operation at the wider community level (Knack, 1999; Portes and Landholt, 1996). An exclusive focus on group interests to the neglect of wider public interests can promote socially destructive "rent-seeking" activities (Olson, 1982 and Knack, 1999). In companies, strong ties of trust and mutual obligation may, in some circumstances block information from outside and impede innovation (Kern, 1998 and Uzzi, 1997).

Although ethnic bonds may serve as a "source of adaptive advantage" when immigrant groups first arrive in a new country, exclusive ethnic ties can impede individuals in expanding their contacts with a wider network. Thus, the importance of bridging social capital is underlined where there is considerable diversity of ethnic and other groups.

The downside of some forms of social capital has been recognised.

Particular forms of bonding social capital have the potential to impede social cohesion in certain circumstances. In this respect, social capital is no different from other forms of capital, the use of which may serve different ends – not all necessarily desirable for communities at large. Some highly bonded groups such as, for example, drug cartels, illegal immigrant smuggler groups, mafia operations and terrorist groups can embody high levels of internal trust and reciprocity.[8] Likewise, these same groups can contain individuals with high levels of human capital, using financial and other forms of capital for socially destructive and undesirable purposes. Some forms of exclusive social bridging at the national or regional level may have socially destructive consequences.[9] These examples do not undermine the potential of human or social capital in other cases to generate benefits for all or most members of society. The benefits from most types of social bonding and bridging generally greatly outweigh the negative consequences.

3.3. How do we measure social capital?

Measurement of social capital is difficult. Typically, most available measures of social capital centre around trust and levels of engagement or interaction in social or group activities. Putnam (2000*a*), in his analysis of differences in social capital across US states, has made extensive use of a wide range of cross-sectional and longitudinal data sets. His measures of social capital are typically based on a composite index containing the following elements: *i*) intensity of involvement in community and organisational life; *ii*) public engagement (*e.g.* voting); *iii*) community and volunteering; *iv*) informal sociability (*e.g.* visiting friends); and *v*) reported levels of inter-personal trust.

Measurement of social capital is still in its infancy...

In principle, measures of social capital should be *i*) as comprehensive as possible in their coverage of key dimensions (networks, values and norms); and *ii*) balanced between attitudinal or subjective elements on the one hand (*e.g.* reported levels of trust) and behavioural aspects on the other (*e.g.* membership of associations and extent of social ties). The use of such measures should also be related to the cultural context in which behaviour or attitudes related to social capital are measured (*e.g.* the meaning of a survey question on trust may differ considerably across countries).

However the difficulties involved in measuring social capital need to be recognised. Sources, functions and outcomes may be confused in the desire to measure. Much of what is relevant to social capital is tacit and relational, defying easy measurement or codification. Individual attitudes (*e.g.* trust) or behaviour (*e.g.* joining organisations and voting) provide proxy measures of social capital, but these measures should not be confused with the underlying concept. Attempts to capture key dimensions of how people interact and relate to each other are hampered by the lack of suitable data sources. This in turn reflects the absence of a sufficiently comprehensive range of questions in survey questionnaires, and the fact that surveys are not designed to assess social capital per se. Hence, sources of data on social capital at the international level are difficult to obtain.

The World Bank has developed measures of social capital "from the ground up" in the form of specially designed surveys or modules of existing surveys. For example, Narayan and Pritchett (1998) constructed a measure of social capital in rural Tanzania, using data from the Tanzania Social Capital and Poverty Survey (SCPS). This large-scale survey asked individuals about the extent and characteristics of their associational activity, and their trust in various institutions and individuals. A number of new surveys or survey modules are also presently undergoing development in the United Kingdom and Australia (see Cox and Macdonald, 2000 and Schuller *et al.*, 2001).

... but pilot measurement instruments are being developed.

One way of measuring changes in social capital is through measurement of social dysfunctions or absences of social co-operation. Fukuyama measures changes in social capital through changes in crime, family breakdown and trust. Allied to increasing crime rates is increased "social deviance" (increased incivility and lack of civic spiritedness, etc). In this approach, the focus is on long-term shifts in mores and values as indicators of changes in social capital. However care is needed in using indicators of social dysfunction to measure changes in

One inverse measure of social capital is social dysfunction...

social capital since the full range of causes of social breakdown is not known and social capital is only one potential contributor. Moreover, such approaches risk confusing consequences with sources.

... while the World Values Study provides a direct measure of trust.

Various waves of the World Values Study (in 1981, 1991 and 1996)[10] have been used to test the willingness of respondents to trust others. Respondents were asked "Generally speaking, would you say that most people can be trusted, or that you can't be too careful in dealing with people?". Their responses show large differences in reported levels of trust across OECD Members (see Table 3.1); with cross-country differences relatively stable over time;[11] and with neighbouring countries tending to be clustered suggesting strong cultural and regional antecedents of trust.

Table 3.1. **A measure of trust (World Values Study), 1995-96**
Percentage of people saying that most people can be trusted

OECD Members

Norway	65.3	Italy*	35.3
Sweden	59.7	Belgium*	33.2
Denmark*	57.7	Austria*	31.8
Netherlands*	55.8	United Kingdom	31.0
Canada*	52.4	Korea	30.3
Finland	47.6	Czech Republic*	30.3
Ireland*	47.4	Spain	29.8
Japan	46.0	Mexico	28.1
Iceland*	43.6	Hungary*	24.6
Germany	41.8	France*	22.8
Switzerland	41.0	Portugal*	21.4
Australia	39.9	Turkey	6.5
United States	35.6		

Selected non-OECD members

India	37.9	South Africa	18.2
Chile	21.9	Argentina	17.5
Nigeria	19.2	Brazil	2.8

*   1990-91 data
1. The question posed in the survey was: "Generally speaking, would you say that most people can be trusted, or that you can't be too careful in dealing with people?"
Source: World Values Study and Knack and Keefer (1997).

The measure of trust needs to be interpreted cautiously.

One difficulty with such questionnaire measures is that it is not clear if respondents interpret the meaning of "trust" or "most people" in the same way across countries, cultures and time. Also, a distinction needs to be drawn between dispositions of individuals to trust others in general and regardless of context, and the dispositions of individuals to trust persons known to them as distinct from the general "other" (refer to distinction between inter-personal trust among "familiars" and "strangers" above). The particular environment, context and situation are crucial. In countries such as France, Italy and Spain, where inter-personal trust among strangers appears to be low compared to other OECD countries, individuals report high levels of trust in their immediate family circles (according to the World Values Study – see Galland, 1999). Although trust and civic engagement are correlated, Galland finds important differences between different social groups in the way in which individuals exercise their choice of social networks and relations. High levels of trust in one area can co-exist with a restricted radius of engagement or trust in another area. Galland concludes that neither general measures of trust nor civic engagement offer a reliable guide to the quality of social relations or to their interaction at a macro-level. The implication is that the results from a survey like the World Values Study need to be treated cautiously.

Knack and Keefer (1997) also report on an experiment in which a large number of wallets containing $50 were deliberately "lost" in a number of cities. The percentage of "lost" wallets that were returned to their owners in each country had a correlation with the measure of trust of 0.67, providing a tentative indication that people are genuinely more trustworthy in countries with high values of the trust index.[12] Knack and Keefer also constructed a second index, designed to capture the strength of norms of civic co-operation and trustworthiness. The index was obtained by averaging across five questions, addressing the attitudes of the respondents to such things as fraudulent benefit claims and avoidance of fares on public transport. The index showed relatively little variation across OECD countries. Putnam (2000a) shows that in US states, trust is highly correlated with other measures of social capital related to civic engagement and social connectedness. This suggests that trust may be an acceptable proxy for social capital in the absence of a wider and more comprehensive set of indicators.

Trust and civic engagement are likely to be inter-related.

3.4. The sources of social capital

Social capital is built at the "level" of families, communities, firms, and national or sub-national administrative units and other institutions. Typically, the idea of social capital is associated with relations in civil society. However, relationships of trust and networks also involve public organisations and institutions. Social capital is embedded in norms and institutions, which include public and legal entities. The focus of analysis may also extend to different groups within civil society such as gender, occupational, linguistic or ethnical groups. The following sources and dimensions can be identified for the development of social capital: *i*) family; *ii*) schools; *iii*) local communities; *iv*) firms; *v*) civil society; *vi*) public sector; *vii*) gender; and *viii*) ethnicity. Although much attention has been given to the role of voluntary and civic associations, the key roles of families, schools and firms have been relatively neglected in recent debates and analyses of social capital.

Social capital is built up by social groups ranging from the family to the nation.

Families create norms and social ties, and provide a social network that benefits its members – especially in the context of extended families in "familial societies" (see Coleman, 1990 and Bourdieu, 1985, 1979). Relations within the family based on reciprocity and the ability to meet the emotional and physical needs of children can also foster the development of trust and co-operative behaviour outside the immediate family circle. The material and emotional support shared freely between family members can generate an implicit willingness and expectation to reciprocate such support within and outside the family. The family is also a primary source of learning, as well as a potential stimulator of success in formal education. Given that education has potentially strong effects in increasing social capital (see below), the family's role in education adds an indirect positive influence on social capital. Coleman measures social capital in families by indicators of: *i*) physical presence of adults or parents in the household; and *ii*) the quality and intensity of attention paid by adults or parents to children. The ratio of adults to children is also a way of measuring the latter. In general, controlling for other factors,

Families are primary building blocks for social capital.

the more siblings and the lower the number of adults in the house, the less social capital is available to students. However, strong family ties (bonding) may on occasion inhibit wider "bridging" relationships.

Social relations that constitute social capital are more frequently broken when families move residence (Glaeser, 2001). Social capital tends to be lower for children in single-parent families, other things constant. The greater the number of adults in the household, the fewer the children, and the less often a family moves residence, the higher on average is the level and quality of attention given to any one child (McLanahan and Sandefur, 1994 and Hao, 1994). McLanahan and Sandefur review US research to claim that divorce, particularly with often-attendant drops in income, parental involvement with children and access to community resources tend to diminish children's well-being and educational achievement. A number of studies (Biblarz, Raftery and Bucur, 1997 and Simons, 1996) show that residing in single-parent or step-parent homes is correlated with a number of disadvantages for children such as lower rates of school completion, higher rates of criminality and substance abuse and higher rates of teen pregnancy. Painter and Levine (1999) confirm this point: they find, by using longitudinal data for the United States, that the link between family structure and various measures of child well-being seemed to be causal rather than linked to innate characteristics of families at risk. However, these effects may be partially or entirely offset by other factors.[13]

Schools and institutions of learning can also sustain social capital...

Schools can foster values for social co-operation as well as providing "meeting places" where various social networks can intersect. More broadly, institutions of higher education, adult learning and professional associations can foster networks crossing different sectors of learning, enterprise and voluntary initiative. To the extent that teaching methods and organisation of learning encourage shared learning and teamwork as well as openness to new ideas and cultural diversity, the more schools can underpin social capital which bridge across different groups in society.

... as can local communities...

Communities and neighbourhoods also play a role in social capital formation. Social interactions among neighbours, friends and groups generate social capital and the ability to work together for a common good. Coleman (1990) links the family to local community in his analysis of "closure" whereby communities exercise influence over its members through risk of sanctions for non-compliance with certain norms. Loury[14] (1987) discusses social capital as "local public goods" that communities produce. These local public goods may be very general in nature, such as peer influence, contacts, and friendship networks.

... and firms.

Some of the growing literature on the "new economy" (*e.g.* Drucker) emphasises networks, trust, partnerships and collaborative ventures. According to this view, innovation is increasingly based on collaboration, rapid learning and networks. There is a potentially strong growth capacity through innovative networks within and across industries linking suppliers, customers and researchers. Clustering of industries, with all the benefits of collaboration associated with networks, may be correlated with national competitive advantage (Porter, 1990). In this view, ability to "network" or communicate outside formal channels is increasingly important. Taylorist organisations based on formal rules and hierarchical power structures rely less on networking and trust than post-Fordist organisations where authority and management responsibilities are more internalised and where trust and information-sharing are more crucial. Hence, higher skills are needed across the work-force. Informal networks promoting sharing of tacit knowledge are important. Organisations which "learn" to socialise knowledge and skills through more effective forms of interaction, networks and norms of trust and co-operation are important sources of social capital.

Another source of social capital is civil society. Civil society consists of the "groups and organisations, both formal and informal, which act independently of the state and market to promote diverse interests in society".[15] There are impor-tant synergies in the relationship between civil society, state and market. The extent and density of relations among groups can be important for these syner-gies to be effective in promoting well-being and economic growth. In his analysis of social capital in different Italian regions, Putnam (1993) explains differences in economic and political performance among regions in terms of historically acquired social capital in various types of associations and civic traditions. Put-nam stresses the importance of various types of associations between people (groups like sports clubs, co-operatives, mutual aid societies, cultural associa-tions, labour unions, etc.). These groups promote the accumulation of bonding and bridging social capital, with positive impacts including improved efficacy of political institutions. Thus, for Putnam, interactions among people in these groups and organisations create horizontal networks of civic engagement that help participants to act collectively in a way that has an impact on community productivity and well-being. In short, voluntary associations and networks can act like schools in fostering of trust and civic engagement with benefits to other sectors of the society, including the state and market.

Associations and voluntary organisations also play a role.

Public governance based on commitment to public welfare, accountabil-ity and transparency provides a basis for trust and social inclusion, which in turn can strengthen social capital. The political, institutional and legal condi-tions prevailing in a country[16] can underpin networks and norms for social co-operation. These two categories can complement and reinforce each other in promoting well-being. Hence, social capital not only produces better public governance and more effective political institutions, but the latter can comple-ment rather than replace community-based networks and reinforce trust.

Levels of trust, social engagement and types of engagement (formal, informal) can vary considerably between men and women as they face differ-ent social networks and levels of access to information. In some cases, men's networks tend to be more formal since men are more often involved in formal employment, whereas women's networks tend to be more informal and include more kin (Moore, 1990). The capacity of children to trust has roots in the relationship of children with mothers – almost certainly because mothers are very often the primary carers – although the quality of father-child rela-tionship is also important (Amato, 1998, p. 247). Social capital can also be built through active civic, labour market and political participation of women. Discrimination based on gender can therefore have negative effects on the formation of particular forms of social capital.[17]

Gender is a key determinant of access to social capital...

Ethnic ties are another example of how actors, who share common values and culture, can bond together for mutual benefit. Portes and Sensenbrenner (1993) noted that elements such as reciprocity, bounded solidarity, and enforceable trust (the existence of social obligations) were key features of the

... as is ethnicity.

47

relationship between ethnicity and social capital. For immigrant groups, ethnicity serves as a "source of adaptive change" when they first arrive to their new country as they rely on social capital for guidance and multidimensional support. For examples, ethnic groups are sources of financial and human capital for budding entrepreneurs as strong kinship ties encourage loans or grants for business ventures and provide inexpensive labour (Geertz, 1962). Ethnic ties can often provide valuable information on the local labour market. The ties also provide a social safety net by meeting material and financial needs during lean times and caring for children and elders (Abrams and Bulmer, 1986). Of course, ethnicity may serve simultaneously as a way to bind some people together while keeping others apart.

3.5. Are trust and civic participation changing over time?

There is evidence of civic disengagement in some countries but not in others.

Changes in levels of social capital reflect longer-term shifts in norms, values and patterns of social interaction. Putnam (2000a) has pointed to a decline in social and civic engagement in the United States. The declining trend for the United States is not fully matched by evidence for other countries. In the United Kingdom and Sweden, membership of various types of civil organisations has increased in both absolute terms and relative to total population. In some countries (notably Australia), the pattern of civic engagement has changed, becoming more individualistic and transient. Differences in levels of trust and civic engagement by age-cohort are apparent in some countries.

While traditional, locally embedded forms of social connection (families, neighbourhoods and traditional mass organisations) seem to be on the decline in many OECD countries, other forms of social connection, often distant, transitory and more self-interested are also emerging. Whether these new forms of social connection are sufficient to replace the older forms is an open question. Trends and patterns of civic engagement, voting, membership of various types of organisations, levels of trust and informal socialising all provide important clues to emerging trends in OECD countries. This section briefly reviews evidence in a selection of OECD countries (Australia, Germany, France, Japan, the Netherlands, Sweden, the United Kingdom and the United States). More detail is given in Appendix E.

There is little evidence for declining social engagement outside Australia and the United States.

This evidence highlights:

- Stable or rising participation in civic organisations (but not in Australia and the United States).
- Stable or increasing levels of volunteering in most countries.
- Mixed evidence of declining engagement by young people in organisations and volunteering.
- Mixed evidence of declining levels of informal sociability (although the quality and comprehensiveness of data is lacking).
- Mixed evidence of declining levels of political interest and activism.

However, some traditional civic organisations appear to be waning...

- Evidence of declining participation in some traditional forms of civic organisations including trade unions, churches and women's organisations.
- Some evidence of declining inter-personal trust and trust in political institutions (especially among the young in the United Kingdom and the United States).

- New social movements (environmental and other single-issue) have grown in recent decades.

- Membership of cultural and sporting organisations has increased in most countries.

- Shifts in political participation away from face-to-face contact towards contact with professionals and with the media playing a more dominant role.

- Some evidence of shifting engagement towards more informal forms of social connection, which tend to be more individualistic and transient but not necessarily more materialistic or selfish.

- Newer forms of civic participation appear to be narrower and more individualistic, and may be less focussed on collective or group interest or purpose. A type of privatisation of social capital may be at work.

... and new forms of engagement have arisen, particularly single issues groups.

Using cross-national data from the WVS, Inglehart (1997) has also noted declining levels of trust in various types of institutions including political and religious hierarchies. Hence levels of reported confidence or trust in the State, civil service, police, churches as well as in the education system and media, declined for most countries between 1981 and 1990. By contrast, there was relatively little change or even some increase in inter-personal trust in the same period. These trends may be associated with increased levels of educational attainment and a shift in values towards greater personal autonomy and less subservience to authority.

Trust among individuals is up, but trust in public institutions is down.

3.6. What lies behind changes in levels of trust and civic participation?

Is the US and Australian pattern of declining social capital exceptional, or are they anticipating developments for other countries? The evidence indicates that intergenerational impacts are especially strong in the United States. More recent generations (especially those born from the 1950s onwards) are generally less inclined to join, volunteer, vote or engage socially and less inclined to trust others. Putnam (2000a) concludes that the effect of intergenerational differences over time is strong and outweighs the effects of social class, ethnic group or region. He reaches this conclusion by using a variety of data sources, distinguishing between changes that occur in the course of people's lives (civic engagement typically peaks in middle age), differences between cohorts at points different in time (comparing baby boomers with older generations) and finally, differences associated with different periods of time (reflecting the impact of unique or once-off shifts which affect all cohorts).

Intergenerational change is particularly important in the United States.

It is not easy to discover what lies behind these strong intergenerational effects. Putnam considers the impact of World War II in creating a strong national civic spirit, the effects of which stayed with generations born in the period 1910-1940. The resurgence in social capital from the earlier years of the 20th century in the United States (following a period of decline towards the end of the 19th century which has parallels with recent trends) was linked to various civic renewal movements at the turn of the century. Putnam's analysis raises the question of whether the similar patterns observable in Australia are also attributable to similar intergenerational effects, and why they are not so observable in other countries.

Broader shifts are taking place in value systems...

Important shifts are taking place in values, norms and patterns of social behaviour in most OECD countries. Some observers claim (*e.g.* Inglehart, 1997) that these are part of a natural evolution in modern societies towards more personal autonomy, less hierarchical control, lower group and cultural identity and, in some cases, post-materialistic or "post-modern" and individualistic goals. Inglehart (1991) and Yankelovich (1981) also suggest that increased material wealth is a major cause of social turmoil and dysfunction in the initial and middle stages of economic development, while at a later stage of economic development, relative economic security might lead to a return to more traditional values. The implication of these shifts is that social ties may be changing rather than declining.

... sometimes involving a weaker commitment to common causes.

The rise of new values with more emphasis on autonomy and less deference may have some undesirable side effects such as weakened commitment to duty and common enterprise. Where once individuals could fall back on extended families, churches and other social supports, these traditional supports have weakened. One impact is that the transition to adulthood is likely to be more problematic for those in search of identity, beliefs and place in society. In the view of some commentators (for example, Fukuyama, 1999) an erosion in common values, identities and social goals is eroding trust and commitment to high-quality, public-interest civic engagement.

New forms of engagement may be emerging.

Rothstein (1998) argues that people may share less and less the same values and lifestyles, but may be more interested and socially engaged. Using survey data for Sweden, he suggests that individuals are more willing to give support to other individuals but also to accept that they have other, different values and want to engage themselves for different causes. Whether this finding could be replicated in other countries is open to question, but it illustrates a key challenge associated with shifting values and norms. Frequently it will make little sense to attempt to re-create past traditions of engagement, but instead efforts must be concentrated on re-invigorating societies with greater civic and public commitment based on new aspirations and attitudes.

TV watching is linked to reduced civic engagement...

Putnam (2000*a*) finds a strong link between the growing incidence of watching television in the United States (and less selective programme viewing) and declining social engagement, controlling for other factors such as race, social status and age. Strong intergenerational effects, combined with the growing amount of time watching TV, seem to explain the bulk of the decline in social capital in the US since the mid-1960s. De Hart and Dekker (1999) find a link between television-watching and civic disengagement in the Netherlands (not to explain a decline in total social capital but rather why some groups are more engaged than others). They found that persons who watched a lot of TV set aside comparatively little time for visiting friends and acquaintances, community volunteering, receiving visitors at home, conversations with other members of the household, conducting correspondence or telephone calls.[18] Findings such as these raise the question of why, given a global increase in television-watching, decline in social capital is only clearly observable in the United States and perhaps Australia.

... while the impact of the Internet has yet to be fully realised.

As Putnam (2000*a*, p. 170) argues, the timing of the internet revolution makes it difficult to link it as a main cause of change or decline in social capital – especially in the US where the decline began 25 years earlier. Its future impact may be substantial. Importantly, where computer-mediated communication has been deemed positive for sharing information, gathering opinions and debating alternatives among physically distant people, building trust has often been seen as more difficult to achieve in a virtual environment. Instead, communication over the Internet appears to be a complement to face-to-face social interactions rather than a substitute for it.

Putnam argues that in the United States increased working time, double-income families, and urban sprawl are factors in the decline of social capital, but are less significant than intergenerational differences and TV-watching. The shift from multi-use rural neighbourhoods to single-use (residential) urban and suburban areas appears to have reinforced a decline in civic engagement. At the same time, however, Putnam found no evidence that changing patterns of female employment in the paid labour force had much impact on community involvement. Controlling for level of education, marital status and year of birth, Putnam found that US women were more socially engaged than men for all categories of employment (full-time, part-time and non-employed). Women in part-time jobs (especially those who had found a preferred balance of work and family-care) tended to be more socially engaged.[19] A striking conclusion was that declines in community participation in the United States were present for all categories of employment including women not in paid employment, thus indicating that changes in patterns of female employment were not a major factor in declining civic engagement. However, in the United States pressure of time allied to increased working hours may have played some role for both men and women.

Working time and urban sprawl are also factors.

The welfare state has been cited as a possible cause of declining social capital. The argument is that when social obligations become increasingly public in the welfare state, voluntary, familial or inter-personal ties tend to weaken, and people have less incentive to deliver voluntary services (Norton, 1998). An alternative possibility is that welfare state policies, rather than "crowding out" voluntary effort and initiative, can encourage solidarity both symbolically and practically. This may be achieved by reducing the risks individuals face through social protection programmes and by support for skills acquisition as a way to encourage and empower individuals to develop their potential (HRDC, 1999). The evidence in de Hart and Dekker (1999), Rothstein (1998) and Hall (1999) for, respectively, the Netherlands, Sweden and the United Kingdom do not provide support for a "crowding-out" hypothesis. They find that levels of volunteering, informal socialising and participation in community projects are relatively high in these countries and that there is little evidence that these have declined or have been adversely affected by public social policies.

It has been suggested that the welfare state crowds out voluntary initiative and social capital, but the evidence is weak.

In particular, two of the countries with the most extensive welfare policies, the Netherlands and Sweden, also have the highest scores in the amount of unpaid work in voluntary associations according to a survey of eight European countries (Gaskin and Davis Smith, 1995).[20] In response to the question, "In the past year, have you carried out any unpaid work or activity for or with an organisation which has nothing to do with your paid work and is not solely for your own benefit or the benefit of your family?", 36 per cent of the Swedish population answered yes, as compared to an average of 27 per cent across other European countries.

Since the industrial revolution, the role of the nuclear or extended family has declined as both an economic unit of production and as an educator, possibly weakening some family networks. More recent changes in family

Increasing instability in family life may have eroded social capital.

structures and patterns of stability imply that individuals are more likely to use impersonal ties to obtain finance, take care of children and educate them. However, extended family cultural capital can still provide an important social safety net by meeting material and financial needs during difficult times, and assisting in the care of children and elders (Abrams and Bulmer, 1986).

According to projections based on recent patterns (*The State of America's Children, 1998 Yearbook Children's Defense Fund*), 1 in 2 children will live in a single parent family at some point in childhood, 1 in 3 will be born to unmarried parents, 1 in 4 will live with only one parent, 1 in 8 will be born to a teenage mother and 1 in 25 will live with neither parent. Fukuyama identifies family break-up, absent parents and rising individualism as factors corroding trust and contributing to rising social dysfunction. While the longer-term impacts of these changes for the fostering of trust and civic engagement are not clear, they have important implications for social policy as with fewer family ties and ageing populations, there is an increasing risk of social isolation for those in need.

3.7. What is the impact of social capital on well-being?

A variety of benefits flow from higher levels of social connectedness.

Like human capital, social capital provides important benefits to individuals and societies. Some of these benefits, such as higher productivity, are directly economic, and evidence of their impact is reviewed in Section 3.9 below. Evidence for the impact of social capital on other aspects of well-being is reviewed in this section.

A number of studies in various countries have shown that, controlling for initial health status, the extent of social connectedness *i.e.* the degree to which individuals form close bonds with relations, friends and acquaintances – is associated with higher life expectancy.[21] Putnam (2000a) reviews a large number of empirical studies which report a positive link between social capital (largely measured in terms of social networks) and education, child welfare, crime, neighbourhood vitality (*e.g.* resale prices), health (both physical and psychological), happiness, and democratic government. He also reports a strong and significant correlation between measures of social capital at United States state level and a composite measure of child welfare, controlling for characteristics such as race, income and level of initial education.

Social capital is correlated with better health...

Perhaps the most convincing evidence of the positive impact of social ties lies in the area of personal health. Already in the nineteenth century, the sociologist Emile Durkheim found a close link between incidence of suicide and the degree to which individuals are integrated into society. He found that rates of suicide increased in periods of rapid social change. The effect was attributed to disruption of the fabric of society and weakened social connectedness. Putnam (2000a) cites the results of numerous new studies, which indicate a link between social connectedness on the one hand and health and personal well-being on the other (after controlling for social, racial and demographic characteristics of individuals). Longevity also appears to be affected by the extent of social connectedness. He suggests two possible reasons for these links: *i*) social networks furnish tangible assistance and care which reduce psychic and physical stress; and *ii*) social capital might trigger a physiological mechanism stimulating individuals' immune systems to fight disease and buffer stress.

The research on health impacts of social capital shows that social isolation tends to precede illness, reinforcing the view that social isolation is a cause rather than consequence of illness. The psychological literature which spans more than three decades of work, confirms the association between supportive relationships and mental health (*e.g.* Brown and Harris, 1978). Putnam (2000*a*) also reviews some of the evidence on the impact of social capital on self-reported happiness and well-being. Again, a positive link emerges even when controlling for other factors. He observes that "... in study after study, people themselves report that good relationships with family members, friends, or romantic partners – far more than money or fame – are prerequisites for their happiness" (p. 332). Elderly persons living alone and without friends or relatives have a relatively greater risk of developing dementia or Alzheimer's disease, other factors constant. A survey of 1 200 persons over three years carried out by the Stockholm Gerontology Research Centre showed that among other factors, an extensive social network protects against dementia (Fratiglioni *et al.*, 2000). The importance of satisfying contact with others, especially immediate family and children was highlighted. Satisfying contact seemed to protect against dementia even if the contact was relatively infrequent.

... and social isolation is linked to unhappiness and illness.

Rose (2000) showed that, in Russia, measures of connection to others who can be relied on to help, control over what happens to oneself and trust in others explained much of the individual variation in physical and emotional health. The impact of social capital was close to that of household income, and greater than that of the level of education completed. Rose found evidence for strong informal networks between friends, relatives, and other face-to-face groups parallel to the existence of a more distant political and social life in which trust is lower. He claimed that there was stronger reliance on informal social capital than on the formal institutions of the state to deal with problems.

Putnam (2000*a*) reports evidence that measures of social capital are second only to poverty in correlating with the breadth and depth of impact on children's lives.[22] While poverty is associated with higher teenage fertility, mortality and idleness, community engagement has the opposite effect. By contrast, the level of education of the adult population has much less of an impact on child welfare once poverty, social capital and demographic characteristics are controlled for. However, given the known impacts of education on poverty and social capital, these results may not adequately account for the interactive or combined effect of human capital working through various channels including social capital and socio-economic status.

Social capital improves child welfare...

Work by community psychologists shows that child abuse rates tend to be higher in neighbourhoods where cohesion is lower (Korbin and Coulton, 1997). Garbarino and Sherman (1980) study two neighbourhoods with similar income levels and similar rates of working women and single-parent households. Residents in neighbourhoods at greater risk of child abuse were more reluctant to ask for help from neighbours and that parents were less likely to exchange child-care with neighbours or allow their children to play with others. Children in low-risk neighbourhoods were more than three times as likely as children in high-risk areas to find a parent at home after school.

... lowers rates of child abuse...

Runyan and others also found that the social connectedness of mothers was a key factor in successfully avoiding behavioural and emotional problems

... and facilitates the transition to adult life.

53

of children later in life. Aspects of social connectedness included presence of supportive social networks for mothers as well as socially supportive neighbourhoods. They conclude: "the parents' social capital... confers benefits on their off-spring, just as children benefit from their parents' financial and human capital" (Runyan *et al.*, 1998). Families based on relatively close bonds appear to be more likely to "gain a greater degree of compliance and adherence to their values". Trusting relations learned and fostered in families can assist young people in their transition to adulthood and their full civic participation (Teachman, Paasch, and Carver, 1999; and Darling and Steinberg, 1997).

Social capital is also correlated with lower crime...

Social capital is important not only in discouraging anti-social or criminal behaviour but also in positively rewarding and channelling community energies. International evidence linking the World Values Study to results of the *International Crime Victim Survey*[23] (ICVS) suggests that a range of social norms and values associated with social capital may be connected to cross-country differences in rates of criminal victimisation. Halpern (forthcoming) uses data for 18 countries relating values to incidence of crime provided by ICVS and controlling for inequality, GDP per capita and trust. He found, not surprisingly, a significant correlation between crime and "self-interested" attitudes (related to propensity to keeping money found, cheating, lying and avoiding fares on public transport). These attitudes were more prevalent among the young, males and urban dwellers. Two-thirds of cross-national variation in crime rates could be accounted for by means of country-level variables for self-interested values, economic inequality and social trust.[24] He summarises his results by referring to economic inequality as the "motive", social trust as the "opportunity" and "self-interested" values as the means to undertake offending behaviour. While these results relate to country level data at one point in time and do not prove causality, they suggest some potentially important linkages at an aggregate level between aspects of social capital and crime. Kawachi *et al.* (1997) also suggest that a key causal link in the relationship between violent crime, social distrust and inequality is low self-esteem, dignity and social status. Where self-esteem, dignity and social status are undermined by poverty and exclusion, trust and social ties are undermined with negative consequences in terms of ill-health and crime.

US evidence shows that, even controlling for poverty and other factors that might encourage criminal behaviour, communities characterised by *i)* anonymity and limited acquaintance among residents; *ii)* unsupervised teenage peer groups; and *iii)* low level of local civic participation, face an increased risk of crime and violence (Sampson and Morenoff, 1997 and Sampson, 1995). Putnam (2000*a*) argues that the decline in neighbourhood social capital in the United States, as revealed through community monitoring, socialising, mentoring and organising, is an important factor in inner-city decline. Sampson, Raudenbush and Earls (1997) used extensive survey data for Chicago neighbourhoods to show that mutual trust and neighbourly altruism were key factors in explaining inter-neighbourhood differences in crime rates (controlling for neighbourhood economic and social characteristics). Complementing Putnam's observation about the impact of informal social capital on learning outcomes (see Appendix C), their analysis suggests that "individual participation in local organisations, number of neighbourhood-based programs, and extent of kin and friendship ties in the neighbourhood – didn't seem to make much of a difference". Rather, the authors conclude, "reductions in violence appear to be more directly attributable to informal social control and cohesion among residents" (Sampson, Raudenbush and Earls, 1997, pp. 918-924).

The effectiveness of public institutions and government in promoting inclusion and cohesion may depend crucially on social capital. Putnam (1993 and 2000*b*) uses data on voting behaviour, tax cheating and civic and political engagement to show a link from social capital to performance of government institutions. Regions or states with higher levels of trust and engagement tend to have better quality government, even controlling for other social and economic factors. Moreover, individuals who are connected to others by community, occupation or association are less likely to be disengaged in local political activity and to share extremist views. In other words, social and civic skills are fostered in voluntary civic associations – what Putnam refers to as "schools for democracy". Most forms of civic engagement, although not all, help to create trust, reciprocity and co-operation with positive spin-offs for local communities, societies and economies. In civic associations, individuals learn to engage in discussions with others – often of an opposing view.

... linked to better government...

As noted in Chapter 2, a growing literature has focussed on the determinants of "life satisfaction" or subjective well-being. Using survey results, these studies examine the association between levels of reported well-being or happiness and demographic, social, ethnic and other factors. Because of a lack of suitable data which can track individuals over time it is difficult to draw general conclusions. However, a number of pertinent insights have emerged from this literature. Putnam (2000*a*) tracks trends in reported levels of happiness and associated characteristics of individuals (p. 333). He finds that, along with personal health, the single most significant factor appears to be social ties. Marital status is also strongly related to reported happiness. Putnam finds that human and social capital seem to yield increases in happiness at both individual and more aggregate levels.[25] Average regional-level income impacts on well-being much less than education, health or social capital. Holding other things constant, an increase in average income at the US state level does not increase the reported happiness of individuals, whereas state-level increases in human or social capital do.

... and perhaps even more important than human capital in improving well-being.

Evidence from the United States and Britain reviewed by Blanchflower and Oswald (2000) supports the view that social ties may be more important for happiness than education and income – at least for average to above-average levels of income. Myers (1999) finds similar results for the US on the impact of close personal relations and social ties on subjective reporting of quality of life. Blanchflower and Oswald examine the impact of life events on happiness, including marriage, unemployment, divorce, etc. As in Putnam (2000*a*), they find evidence for falling levels of happiness between the early 1970s and the late 1990s. Although education is important as a correlate of happiness, it appears to occupy third place after social ties and health. Income also matters, but not as much as social ties, health or education, and its impact declines at higher levels of income. These results are consistent with the macro-level relationships between levels of GDP per capita and overall levels of well-being reported across countries (Inglehart, 1997).

3.8. The relationship between social capital and social inequality

Acute forms of social exclusion (by social, ethnic, gender or regional status) appear to go hand in hand with lower levels of trust and civic engagement –

especially of the "bridging" type. Groups may be less inclined to co-operate with or trust other groups even when high levels of co-operation and trust prevail within each group. This section addresses two inter-related issues:

- At the micro level, how does social capital interact with social inequality (access to learning, jobs and income)?
- At the macro level, does social capital lead to more equality in income and social opportunity, and does such equality generate higher trust and social connectedness?

Social capital is linked to equality, although the direction of causality is uncertain.

Countries and regions with high levels of trust and civic engagement tend to be more equal in terms of income, adult literacy and access to further learning. The higher the initial endowment of social capital, the more likely is it that individuals will acquire more throughout life. For those on the "inside" of particular networks and communities, there are important means of access to resources from which "outsiders" are excluded. For example, Hall (1999) reports significant differences in types of social engagement in the United Kingdom across social groups (a point also developed in relation to France in Galland, 1999). Hall found that individuals from middle-class backgrounds were more likely to join new associations at frequent intervals, accumulate more memberships over their lifetimes, and join diverse and extensive social networks. Individuals from a working-class background, on the contrary, tended to join fewer associations, often associated with specific tasks, and stayed in them for long periods of time.

Economic inequality may be both cause and consequence of inequality in social capital.

The trends in social capital considered in Section 3.6 may reflect changes in patterns of economic inequality within and across countries. Putnam (2000a, p. 360) claims that decline in social capital in the US is linked to growing inequality of income and wealth. The direction of causation may be working in both directions, as he also reports evidence that inequality and lower civic engagement tend to reinforce each another. Knack (1999) also finds a positive correlation between equality of income and trust at the cross-country level. However, Fukuyama (1999) adopts a rather different view, arguing that family break-up and the decline in trust which tends to result from it has been responsible for some of the increase in US poverty.

There is uncertain evidence on the links between social exclusion, social capital and inequalities in health.

Using state-level data from the US General Social Survey, Kawachi *et al.* (1997) argue that income inequality lowers social capital and through this channel leads to higher mortality rates (as well as higher rates of crime). In addition to the mediating role of social capital, there are, of course, direct linkages between poverty and ill-health. The key insight from their analysis is that income distribution at state level matters more than average income for health outcomes.[26] This is supported by Wilkinson (1996) and others, who report that health inequality within countries or regions is more closely linked to inequality than to average income levels. Halpern and Nazroo (2000) also suggest that individuals from ethnic minority groups experience better mental health and personal well-being when living in areas of high group concentration. However, Lynch *et al.* (2000) warn against "overly simplistic interpretations of the links among social capital, economic development, public policy and health". Moreover, Muntaner *et al.* (2000) believe that the public health utility of the concept of social capital may have been exaggerated since the concept has been "portrayed narrowly and focused on more optimistic appraisals of its relevance to population health". Accordingly, to these critiques, the limited conceptualisation and empirical evidence, which social capital is based on, calls for caution.

Countries polarised along lines of class, ethnicity or language (Collier, 1998; Knack and Keefer, 1997) almost inevitably face a higher risk of social fragmentation. However, many multi-racial and linguistically diverse societies have proved to be able to manage and harness diversity with positive outcomes. For example, comparing different countries, La Porta *et al.* did not find a significant correlation between ethno-linguistic heterogeneity and reported mistrust.

Social capital can act either to entrench social fragmentation, or to cross the divides.

Although the fragmentation of social relations may lead to the formation of new patterns and networks, which should be welcomed, the risk is that new forms of social capital may be unevenly shared. While the effect of the Internet may offer both hopes and challenges, it must be weighted against the risks of social inequality of access to cyberspace, its perceived impersonal nature, further fragmentation of people into distinct groupings, and being a possible tool of passive, private entertainment. This situation may be compounded in the future as some groups are likely to have access to new technologies and forms of learning linked to enhanced labour market opportunities.

Willms (2001), using Canadian data on student achievement, finds that individuals from poor backgrounds who also live in poor communities are especially vulnerable to low educational achievement. Communities with high levels of social and cultural capital can achieve higher learning outcomes. Willms stresses the importance of disciplinary climate, parental involvement and high expectations in raising school and literacy standards. Furthermore, family and community effects are important in raising the skills and literacy of disadvantaged adults. These findings also suggest that the responses of societies to disadvantage are an important determinant of how well they perform in terms of overall literacy. Cross-country differences in adult literacy and skill levels greater for lower socio-economic groups. This suggests that a key element in strategies to improve overall literacy standards is the identification of the needs of the socially disadvantaged, especially those with poor access to social networks.

Social capital can mediate differences in overall literacy or learning outcomes.

3.9. Impact of social capital on economic well-being

3.9.1. *Productivity in firms and organisations*

Trust underwrites transactions whether they are private, social, economic or political in nature. Central to the definition of social capital is the concept of networks.[27] Firms can benefit from norms of co-operative trust embodied in various types of intra-firm or inter-firm networks because these facilitate co-ordination and lower transaction costs arising from negotiation and enforcement, imperfect information and layers of unnecessary bureaucracy.[28] In this perspective, trust has many dimensions including a belief in the good intentions of others as well as their competence and reliability.

Trust has a role in facilitating productivity...

Humphrey and Schmitz (1998) highlight how "trust-based relations between economic agents have been seen as part of the competitive advantage of manufacturing enterprises in Germany, Japan and parts of Italy...". Suppliers and buyers can sustain long-term relations of co-operation and

... when embodied in the organisational culture of firms...

57

mutual obligation through repeated transactions forged on trust and networking. Business networks covering marketing, training, or research can generate long-term benefits by reducing overhead costs, sharing information and imposing sanctions on opportunistic behaviour. In some niche markets, such as in software development or the garment industry, entrepreneurs can take advantage of economies of time, by sharing information, and adapting quickly to changing demands of customers (Uzzi, 1996 and 1997).

... and may lead to larger and more effective production units...

Some of the research has explored the notion of generalised versus specialised trust. La Porta *et al.* (1997) found that the revenues of the 20 largest firms as a percentage of GDP is positively associated with trust in people in general, and negatively associated with trust in family. They hypothesise that larger firms might prevail more in societies where trust is higher and penalties for opportunistic behaviour are less necessary. By contrast, on the same hypothesis larger firms would be more difficult to develop in closely knit societies based on bonds of family or ethnicity. In this model, trust tends to be an exogenous factor shaped by historical and cultural factors and acting to facilitate collective action and co-operation, including higher civic engagement and government effectiveness.

... as well as enhanced co-operation within firms.

Similarly, intra-firm networks and co-operative norms can facilitate teamwork, enhance efficiency and quality as well as improve the flow of information and knowledge. Shimada (1988) identifies co-operative attitudes among the workers and management as the basic reason for the (historically) strong competitiveness of Japanese automobile companies: "In a US company, each worker is eager to make his individual success, and unwilling to tell what he knows to his colleague. But here, everybody is willing to tell what he knows as much as possible to the colleague. This is because he believes that he can make a success only as a team, not on his own" (Omori, 2001). Different types of social and organisational capital may be more or less relevant at different phases of economic development – witness the decline in the competitiveness of Japanese automobile manufacturing in the 1990s.

3.9.2. *Productivity in regions and neighbourhoods*

Social capital can facilitate regional systems of innovation.

Regional industrial systems based on local learning networks are potentially more flexible and dynamic than those in which learning is confined to individual firms. Regional or local learning networks can allow for information flows, mutual learning and economies of scale. Putnam (2000*a*) contrasts the impact of Silicon Valley and *Route* 128 in the US. He cites Silicon Valley in California where a group of entrepreneurs helped by research effort in the local universities, contributed to the development of a world centre of advanced technology. He comments that "The success is due largely to the horizontal networks of informal and formal co-operation that developed among fledgling companies in the area". By contrast, in the *Route* 128 corridor outside Boston, lack of inter-firm social capital led to a more traditional form of corporate hierarchy, secrecy, self-sufficiency, and territoriality.

3.9.3. *Job search*

Access to social capital helps people to find jobs.

Barbieri, Russell and Paugam (1999) show that, in a number of European countries, social capital is a valuable resource for finding employment, especially in open and flexible labour markets. More than the number of social connections available to an individual, successful job search hinges on the range of persons with whom the individual is connected with and can rely on. Bridging as distinct from bonding social capital is an important asset for individuals in search of employment. However, the unemployed experience less access to extensive, job-based networks and contacts.

A number of economists including Granovetter (1973) have emphasised the role of casual acquaintances, as well as close friends and families, in finding jobs. In a similar vein, Burt (1992) emphasises the absence of close ties[29] as a factor in encouraging mobility of individuals and sharing of knowledge. In closed or dense networks, information becomes more readily redundant. He identifies *information* and *influence* (over one's own autonomy or that of others) as two types of benefits flowing from social networks. A third type of benefit may be identified in the form of *social solidarity* involving co-operation, a sense of social duty and reciprocity not founded on any immediate payback for those contributing to the welfare of others. Loury (1987), one of several independent "inventors" of the concept of social capital, did so to capture the fact that even if the human and financial capital advantages of white Americans were cancelled out, their richer connections to mainstream American institutions would confer an advantage on them relative to middle-class members of minority communities.

3.9.4. Macro-economic benefits

As Arrow (1972) noted, interpersonal trust and norms of trust toward institutions may be central to many economic and social activities. However, analysis of the role of social capital in explaining cross-country differences in economic growth has been limited to date, reflecting the relative novelty of the concept, its heterogeneous nature, and the difficulty of collecting adequate indicators on a cross-country basis. In addition, difficult measurement issues arise when it comes to the question of aggregation.

Depending on the selection of countries, the time period chosen and the inclusion of other explanatory variables in the growth equations, results bearing on the macro-economic effect of social capital have been mixed. Using World Values Study data, Knack and Keefer (1997) found that a measure of general inter-personal trust is positively correlated with growth in GDP when controlling for initial income per head, a human capital variable, and the relative price of investment goods.[30] Using the same data source, Hjerrpe (1998) also found a positive and significant relationship between measures of trust and economic growth for a sample of 27 countries (including a number of middle to low-income countries)[31] after controlling for physical capital, openness to trade and the proportion of the adult population with tertiary education. Yet, Helliwell (1996) found a negative correlation between trust and growth in total factor productivity in a sample of 17 OECD Members.

Recent evidence of the impact of trust on economic growth has been mixed...

Other researchers have suggested that trust can stimulate savings, risk-taking and investment. Guiso *et al.* (2000) report that in Italian regions with high levels of social trust, households invest less in cash and more in stock, use more cheques, have higher access to institutional credit, and make less use of informal credit. Firms also have more access to credit and are more likely to have multiple shareholders. The effect of trust appears stronger in regions where legal enforcement is weaker and among less-educated people. The financial behaviour of individuals who have moved from another region is mainly affected by the level of trust in the environment where they live, and in lesser part, by the level of trust prevailing in the province from which they migrated.

Analysis at the sub-national level seems to reveal more by implicitly controlling for some of the confounding contextual and cultural factors. Northern Italy shows significantly better levels of governance, institutional performance, and economic development when other factors were controlled for.[32] Putnam (1993) and Helliwell and Putnam (1999a) argued that stronger social capital enabled the north to take advantage of regional reform to grow more rapidly than the south. To do so, they undertook comparisons of northern and southern Italy, finding evidence of a relationship between inter-regional performance since the mid-1980s and increasing citizen satisfaction with regional governments in the north of the country following reforms in the 1970s.[33] Up to the early 1980s, levels of real GDP per capita were tending to converge in the different Italian regions. Since then, regional differentials have widened again.

... as is any link between group membership and economic growth.

The link between national levels of group membership and economic growth is also unclear. Putnam (1993) found a connection between levels of civic engagement and economic development over a long period of time. He argues that in daily interactions structured by civic associations, people learn trust, social norms, and effective networks for public action. Civic associations can create a dense horizontal network and many opportunities to acquire the social capital of trust.

Other studies have generated inconclusive results suggesting that the proxy data may not be capturing important dimensions of social capital. Knack and Keefer (1997), using indicators of group membership drawn from the World Values Study, found that associations whose functions are to advance their members interests – such as trade unions, political parties and professional associations – had little relation to growth or investment rates. They also found that many other types of associations, such as religious or church organisations, education, arts, music or cultural activities, showed no relation to economic growth but a significant *negative* relation with investment.

It is therefore not obvious that changes in group membership or other forms of social interaction have impacted on recent differences in economic growth across OECD countries. For example the evidence for declining levels of group and civic participation in the United States stands alongside rapid increases in income per capita.

Other research suggests that social infrastructure is important to economic growth.

Much recent work has been concerned with the short-term determinants of economic growth. Other research suggests that countries tend to achieve higher long-term levels of output per worker if they combine high rates of investment in physical and human capital with a high-quality "social infrastructure"[34] (see Hall and Jones, 1999). The quality of "social infrastructure" is primarily related to the effectiveness of institutions and government policies that make up the economic environment within which individuals and firms make investments, create and transfer ideas, and produce goods and services. It is closely related to political, institutional and legal conditions (PIL) described in Chapter 1.

Understanding the limitations of the research is important.

Care is needed in interpreting the role of trust in cross-country economic growth equations. Trust may well be determined by, or correlated with, other aspects of societies that are omitted from the growth regressions. For instance, it may be that corruption or weak legal enforcement lowers trust and, for quite independent reasons, the growth rate. As Knack and Keefer (1997) note, trust might even be a product of optimism in societies that are performing well in economic terms. Poverty and low economic development may hinder the development of trust because people who are economically insecure, or who live in a society of economic under-development and insecurity, may have a lower incentive to trust others.

Some of the impact on macro-economic performance may also be indirect through higher rates of investment in physical and human capital and enhanced performance of "social infrastructure" (or PIL according to Chapter 1). La Porta *et al.* (1997)[35] and Knack and Keefer (1997) report evidence on associations between trust and indicators of government performance, including the effectiveness of the judiciary and the quality of the bureaucracy. However, these studies report a weak association between trust and economic growth (over 1970-1993) but stronger association between a wide variety of outcomes, such as level of education and investment in physical capital using a number of controls. They also report a positive correlation between levels of education and trust, other things equal.[36]

3.10. Conclusion

Care is needed in drawing conclusions from studies that rely on highly aggregate or undifferentiated proxy measures of social capital. However, this chapter has shown that social capital is likely to have positive economic, social and personal benefits based on a wide range of empirical studies in a number of countries.

In conclusion, social capital appears to have economic and social benefits...

There is also a two-way relationship between social capital and human capital. There is a positive association even at a cross-country level, for example, between civic engagement and trust on the one hand, and levels of education on the other.[37]

... and human and social capital may be mutually reinforcing.

It is more difficult to demonstrate a clear link between social capital and economic growth. As in the case of human capital, the evidence is affected by the quality and breadth of proxy measures, the complexity of inter-relationships between different conditioning factors and the difficulty in comparing countries with widely differing cultural, institutional and historical traditions. As Temple (2001) has suggested, this would be a fruitful area for further research.

Although the research is suggestive, there is as yet no robust evidence that social capital is generally related to economic growth.

The evidence reviewed here of the benefits of access to social capital is sufficiently impressive to establish social capital as a dimension to be explored when looking at policies for dealing with poverty and social exclusion – indeed the very term social exclusion implies the denial of access to social capital.

Weak access to social capital is also clearly an important dimension of social exclusion.

Notes

1. De Tocqueville (1835) wrote: "The Americans combat individualism by the principle of interest rightly understood" where he claimed, for example, that "they show with complacency how an enlightened regard for themselves constantly prompts them to assist each other, and inclines them willingly to sacrifice a portion of their time and property to the welfare of the State".

2. Durkheim saw society as composed of "organs" (social facts), or social structures, that had a variety of functions for society.

3. Weber focused on individuals and patterns and regularities of action. He was primarily concerned with action that clearly involved the intervention of thought processes (and the resulting meaningful action) between the occurrence of a stimulus and the ultimate response.

4. Jacobs (1961) defines social capital as "neighbourhood networks".

5. The World Bank's preferred definition of social capital is that it "refers to the institutions, relationships, and norms that shape the quality and quantity of a society's social interactions. Increasing evidence shows that social cohesion is critical for societies to prosper economically and for development to be sustainable. Social capital is not just the sum of the institutions which underpin a society – it is the glue that holds them together" (refer to *www.worldbank.org/poverty/scapital/whatsc.htm*).

6. Some writers on social capital would also incorporate a consideration of "beliefs" into the definition. For example, Adler and Kwon (2000) describe "beliefs" as shared strategic visions, interpretations and systems of meaning. "Beliefs" are close to value orientations which underpin co-operation.

7. Putnam (1993) gives the example that "members of Florentine choral societies participate because they like to sing, not because their participation strengthens the Tuscan social fabric".

8. The examples given do not imply that all or most highly bonded groups have a negative social impact. For example, some forms of bonding such as in families or ethnic groups can have positive health and employment effects which spillover to other groups.

9. Exclusive forms of social bridging may include forms of extreme or totalitarian ideologies.

10. It has carried out representative national surveys of the basic values and beliefs of publics in more than 65 societies. It builds on the European Values Surveys, first carried out in 1981-89. A second wave of surveys, designed for global use, was completed in 1990-1993, a third wave was carried out in 1995-1997 and a fourth wave took place in 1999-2000. For further details, see *wvs.isr.umich.edu/index.html*.

11. Over time, measures of trust seem to be fairly stable for the twenty countries reporting trust in 1981 and 1990 (with a correlation coefficient of 0.91).

12. This correlation cannot be attributed to a possible confounding effect of higher per capita incomes: the partial correlation between trust and wallets returned, controlling for per capita income, was higher than the simple correlation.

13. Some caution with these results is necessary, given that lone parenthood is highly correlated with many other indicators of disadvantage. For example, Joshi *et al.* (1999) found that children of lone mothers who had broken up with the child's father did not fare worse educationally or behaviourally than other children when current income and educational attainment of the mother are controlled for.

14. Loury is primarily concerned with the inequality of social capital and its capacity to affect the socio-economic class structure.

15. This definition is used by the World Bank at *www.worldbank.org/poverty/scapital/sources/civil*1.*htm*

16. Referred to under the acronym PIL in Chapter 1.

17. Picciotto (1998) remarks "Gender discrimination squanders trust, hinders family relations, restricts social networks, and depletes social capital, the valuable capacity of societies to work toward common goals".

18. De Hart and Dekker also found that this relationship remains present even when the effects of education level or sex of the respondent, age or income level are controlled for.

19. However, non-employed women were more engaged than full-time.

20. Other countries with high unpaid work in voluntary associations include Belgium, Bulgaria, Germany, Ireland, Slovakia and the United Kingdom.

21. However, as a potential downside of social capital, not all forms and degrees of social ties may necessarily promote health. Some social ties may be oppressive or associated with unhealthy behaviour.

22. These results hold up even when controls are used for income, level of education, racial composition and family structure in each state.

23. The ICVS relates to surveys of victims of all types of crime as distinct from reported crime. These surveys took place in 1989, 1992 and 1996. Refer to *ruljis.leidenuniv.nl/group/ifcr/www/icvs/index.htm*

24. A curious result of his empirical investigation is that social trust is associated with higher levels of crime, when inequality and self-interest are controlled for. This finding may reflect a supply of "victims" at a given level of inequality and self-interest. Victims continue to trust by leaving doors and cars open in spite of the untrustworthy behaviour of others.

25. Putnam (2000*a*) does not find any local area (US county) level impact of social capital on happiness although an individual impact still holds. This may stem from measurement error associated with smaller country-level samples.

26. For an alternative view of the role of social capital in mediating the impact of poverty and inequality on health, see Lynch *et al.* (2000). They claim that the impact of social capital on health may have been exaggerated.

27. "Where people are trusting and trustworthy, and where they are subject to repeated interactions with fellow citizens, everyday business and social transactions are less costly" (Putnam, 2000*a*, p. 288).

28. Fukuyama (1999) defines a network as "as a group of individual agents that share informal norms or values beyond those necessary for ordinary market transactions".

29. What Burt refers to as structural holes.

30. Knack and Keefer find that a one standard deviation change in the trust index is associated with a change in the growth rate of 0.56 of one standard deviation. In alternative terms, a level of trust that is ten percentage points higher (slightly less than one standard deviation) is associated with an annual growth rate that is higher by 0.8 percentage points.

31. Non-OECD countries included were Argentina, Brazil, Chile, China and Russia.

32. Putnam used aggregate time-series data for 20 Italian regions covering the period 1960 to the mid-1980s.

33. Their measure of social capital includes: incidence of newspaper reading, the number of sports and cultural organisations, turnout in referenda, the incidence of preference voting and regional government performance.

34. Their measure of social infrastructure for a large number of developing countries is related to *i*) institutions that favour production over diversion; *ii*) openness to international trade; *iii*) existence of the rule of law and property rights; *iv*) presence of an international language; and *v*) distance from the equator.

35. The authors find that across countries, a one-standard deviation increase in the same measure of trust increases judicial efficiency by 0.7 of a standard deviation and reduces government corruption by 0.3 of a standard deviation.

36. Knack and Keefer report a strong correlation (r = 0.83) between trust and an estimate of average years of schooling for 1980, and note that "education may strengthen trust and civic norms, for example, if ignorance breeds distrust, or if learning reduces uncertainty about the behaviour of others, or if students are taught to behave cooperatively" (p. 1270).

37. For example, rising demand for education associated with changing labour market conditions may not be paralleled by increases in social capital.

Chapter 4

POLICY IMPLICATIONS AND FURTHER RESEARCH NEEDS

"Whatever the difficulties in the design and evaluation of education, there is a genuine policy instrument, or scores of them, right at hand. There are education ministers, and they have tasks and budgets. But make yourself the Minister of Social Capital and who would you talk to when you came to work in the morning? Social capital is itself a bridging concept." Helliwell (2001).

4.1. Introduction

This report suggests that policy makers should be concerned about human and social capital for four main reasons:

Human and social capital contribute both to growth and well-being.

1. There is robust evidence that human capital is an important determinant of economic growth, and while the effect of social capital on growth is unproven, there is enough evidence to justify further research on that possibility.

2. There is evidence that both human and social capital are associated with a wide range of non-economic benefits, including improvements in health and a greater sense of well-being. Such findings are particularly important when set in the context of evidence that, in recent years, average self-reported well-being has not been growing in OECD countries in line with GDP.

3. Social and human capital can be mutually reinforcing.

4. Flowing from the preceding points, the significance of human and social capital for individual life chances is so great that the promotion of social inclusion must take account of both types of capital.

Human and social capital enable individuals, communities, firms and societies to cope with the demands of rapid social and economic change – teaching children to cope with a changing world, reskilling adults for new types of work and providing the trust and sense of common purpose on which most social and economic activities depend. Such capital represents a key resource for sustainable development.

While education and training institutions play a significant role in developing human capital, wider social support for those institutions is critical to their success. Human and social capital are created, formally and informally, in the workplace, in local communities and within families. Social capital resides in social relationships entered into voluntarily, implying that governments will often be facilitating or supporting the development of social capital, rather than actively creating it. Moreover social and human capital are mutually reinforcing. For all these reasons, the policy ideas advanced here are not just addressed to governments, but also to a range of other actors and

Sustaining human and social capital is a matter for everyone – and certainly not just for government.

institutions – such as employers, people working in voluntary organisations, and key public sector workers. Everyone has a part to play.

4.2. Policies for human capital

Policies for human capital need to be set in context.

Policies for human capital need to recognise that:

- Economic change – particularly the increased knowledge-intensity of economic activity – may be changing the demand for human capital, particularly by increasing the emphasis on some non-cognitive skills such as teamwork and innovation.[1]

- All learning environments – including the family, the workplace, and the pre-school environment – are important.

- Partnership and dialogue – between private, public and voluntary sectors – is essential, as is policy co-ordination – linking education to policies for employment and social protection.

- There are substantial differences in both access to, and take up of, further education and training. Policies for lifelong learning need to address these variations if they are to successfully tackle social exclusion.

- Long time scales are often involved, both in the development and erosion of human and social capital.

The research on human capital reviewed here, when set in the context of other research studies and policy development work, has some direct policy implications, and suggests some policy options worthy of further consideration. They are as follows:

This report suggests some policy options for human capital development.

1. *Investments in human capital generate significant private and social benefits.* The latest research reinforces the view that human capital plays a significant role in economic growth. In addition, there is much evidence of significant non-economic benefits flowing from investment in human capital – better health, improved well-being, better parenting, and more social and political engagement. Changes in the structure of the economy are also increasing the demand for skills, as economic activity becomes more knowledge-intensive, and human capital is increasingly central to the competitive edge of firms and nations. These findings do not imply that all investment in education is desirable, but they do provide strong support for the view that wisely-targeted investment in human capital formation represents a sensible public policy choice.

2. *Social capital is linked to educational attainment, suggesting that most forms of education and training could be assisted by various types of community-based networks.* Partnerships are needed to provide people with the platform of readiness and support for learning, recognising that such a platform is often largely the product of home and family environments.[2]

3. *Incentives for continual learning need to be developed.* There may be a case for re-considering the organisation of learning opportunities throughout the lifecycle as well as financial and tax incentives for learning so that the needs of individual learners are better served. There is a need to encourage, and rigorously evaluate, innovative forms of co-financing, such as individual learner accounts (ILAs). Incentives for on-the-job

training, part-time further education, alternation of work and study and use of distant and IT-based learning for adults might be considered.

4. *Curricula and teaching methods need to give weight to inter-personal and other non-cognitive skills alongside cognitive skills.* Effective organisations are, increasingly, learning and innovating organisations. This change is increasing the demand for teamworking ability, flexibility and the capacity to innovate and manipulate knowledge (see OECD, 2001, Chapter 4).

5. *Human capital investment can also help to develop social capital.* Greater emphasis on group-centred problem-solving might help prepare students for more co-operative behaviour. Educational institutions might also be used to promote the strength of local communities, taking advantage of the fact that large proportions of the community have links with such institutions. Community activities can take advantage of the times of the year or day when school premises are not being used for their normal purposes. [Scenario 3, in Chapter 5 of *Education Policy Analysis* (OECD, 2001) describes the role which schools might play in this context.]

6. *Training schemes need to target those most vulnerable to exclusion from the labour market.* Typically, those with the greatest need are least likely to participate in training. Increasing inequalities in income in many OECD countries in recent decades may be further compounded as new forms of learning and technology develop. Changed interventions will be necessary to overcome these problems – for example to ensure that the digital divide does not create unacceptable inequalities of access to distance learning.

4.3. Policies for social capital

The evidence reviewed here shows that social capital is important for well-being, health, and job search activities, and has offered some suggestive evidence regarding its potential role in supporting economic growth. Despite this, some forms of social capital are undesirable – notably that involved when people co-operate for anti-social purposes. Policies need to take account of the diverse forms of social capital and its varying desirability.

Access to social capital is generally beneficial...

As indicated above, the role of government in sustaining social capital is less clear than in the case of human capital. It may often have the role of facilitator, rather than main actor. At the same time, government and other public agencies have a diffuse, but collectively powerful influence on social capital formation. Agencies whose actions have influence on social capital are spread throughout government and the voluntary and private sectors. Local and regional levels of government will often have particularly important roles.

... but the role of government in sustaining social capital is less clear than in the context of human capital...

The main significance of social capital for social exclusion policies is the recognition that access to social capital helps to determine life chances. Specific types of social capital may also be particularly relevant to social exclusion – in particular, "bridging" social capital which refers to social connections which cross boundaries of social class, ethnicity and gender. Crossing such bridges to join the key social networks of access and influence may be critical to the success of immigrant and ethnic minority communities. One option

---

> Box 4.1. **Policies for social capital: some examples**
>
> Policies for social capital are not new. Some examples of policies which depend on social capital for their impact, or act to enhance social capital, are given below:
>
> *Strengthening communities and families to support children in Italy.* In Pistoia, Italy, the municipal government provides children's meeting places, providing support for families not in need of full-time childcare. Parents, grandparents and other family members can attend enrichment activities at these locations, which serve as community meeting points for adults as well as a source of play and experimentation for children. These children's meeting places also serve as after-school environments for school-age children, and as educational resource centres for teachers from the city's *scuole dell'infanzia* and elementary schools.
>
> *Building bridges through community involvement in Northern Ireland.* Ulster People's College, a voluntary organisation in Belfast, provides structured training programmes at a variety of levels for local people involved in voluntary and community work. The college's community leadership programmes helps active community members to become more effective in their work, while the college also acts as a very effective network for community and voluntary workers in Belfast. It is an explicit part of the college's mission to involve people from both nationalist and unionist communities and to contribute towards peace and reconciliation in Northern Ireland.
>
> *Innovation through networking in Denmark.* Denmark has a number of programmes whose objective is to stimulate innovation through linkages between established research centres and the private sector. Public-private partnerships in research have been encouraged through new legislation on inventions and new rules for private sector financial involvement in public research institutions. Innovation, partnership and networking are also stimulated through "centre contracts" whereby businesses, technological service institutions, and scientists work together on commercially oriented R&D projects, with a mix of government and private sector funding.

might be to target attempts to improve social capital at areas or communities which can be identified as lacking social capital.

Some examples of existing policies which bear on social capital are given in Box 4.1. The new research on social capital lends significance to such initiatives by demonstrating that social contacts acquired in one context can be utilised for a very wide variety of purposes. This means, for example, that participative sports may be seen as having wider benefits, beyond physical health and the pleasure of the activity.

... while research on social capital is still at an early stage.

Research on social capital is at an early stage of development and cannot yet tell us with any degree of confidence whether any given programme or policy will fail or succeed in realising its social capital objectives. At the same time our understanding of social capital and its policy value can only be developed through policy development and evaluation. The options presented below should therefore be seen as ideas worthy of further development, pilots and evaluation, rather than as programmes for which there already exists substantial research support.

Some policy ideas might be piloted and evaluated.

1. *Support for families.* Policy options include the provision of fiscal support, flexibility in working hours and arrangements to encourage or facilitate more parental involvement in the lives of children. Flexibility to allow for more time off for parents and better planning and scheduling of working hours may help – recognising that such family-friendly policies have the joint effect of helping parents who do work,

and encouraging more parents, particularly women, to enter the labour market if they so desire.

2. *Support for voluntary initiatives.* Policy options include both demand-side measures to encourage funding of organisations which make effective use of volunteers, and supply-side measures which encourage employers to offer time off for some sorts of community activity.

3. *Government decision-making processes.* Democracy which involves people is not only a means of making better decisions, but also a critical element in the whole social fabric. Empowerment of citizens and proximity of government to the people can help invigorate local communities and tap into valuable social energy for positive action.

4. *ICT and social capital.* New forms of ICT, alongside more traditional media, can be used to help connect people to their local neighbour-hoods as well as more distant communities. ICT offers new opportunities for government to consult and communicate with citizens, and to open up its own actions to public scrutiny. Electronic networks can also serve to communicate information and ease market transactions, especially where matching information is lacking.[3] Greater opportunities for informal learning, including distance learning, are opened up by new media. It is important that disadvantaged groups have greater access to new media so that they can take fuller advantage of new information highways and networks. Informal environments are becoming increasingly important as countries move towards diverse, demand-led and individualised forms of learning.

5. *Linking health care to communities.* Planning of health care and provision at the local community level, where the elderly and other groups can stay closer to their families and communities, may offer another way of sustaining social ties and reaping positive health benefits which the research has shown are linked to social capital.[4]

4.4. Knowledge gaps and future areas of research

This report has been wide-ranging, and has identified a large number of lines of enquiry for further research. Any list of proposals will inevitably be highly selective. The most salient gaps in our knowledge and understanding appear to lie in the following areas:

1. Extending the measurement of human capital – in particular the direct measurement of competencies beyond the areas of numeracy and literacy into fields such as teamwork, problem-solving and ICT skills. While such competencies, or some dimensions of those competencies, may be dependent on cultural contexts, better measures will still be important, even where, for example, international survey instruments are inappropriate. Current development activities include continuing efforts to build on the *International Adult Literacy Survey* (IALS) to cover a wider range of adult lifeskills.

2. Obtaining a clearer understanding of how demand for human capital is changing and will continue to change, both quantitatively and qualitatively. This will be critical in guiding current initiatives both in training the knowledge workers for the new economy, and in addressing the problems faced by those with few or outdated basic skills. Further work may be needed to integrate thinking about the changing demands

Further work would be useful on the measurement of human capital, how demand is changing and how human and social capital are linked.

for skills with the structure of school curricula and the balance between initial formal education and lifelong learning.

3. Clarifying the links between human and social capital to explore how social networks can promote the education of individuals and how education can promote social capital.

Further research could clarify the concept of social capital, and develop better measures.

4. Furthering conceptual development of the idea of social capital, preferably by linking such development to empirical work. It will also involve further developing our taxonomy of different forms of social capital, and identifying the fields of analysis and forms of social capital where application of the concept is most fruitful.

5. Developing better measures of social capital in social groups, as well as, separately but linked, improved measures for individual access to social capital. A number of survey instruments are being developed for these purposes. Measures used in Putnam (2000a) relate to patterns of behaviour or attitude recorded in surveys of individuals. Reported dispositions to trust or reported activities relating to informal socialisation, voting behaviour, joining in various types of organisations and volunteering for community projects provide important indicators of norms and patterns of network behaviour in the population at large.

We also need to identify the policies that work.

6. Through policy evaluation, gaining a better understanding of what works in promoting social capital, and the contexts in which the promotion of social capital yields most benefits. Some ideas on areas ripe for evaluation have been suggested above.

4.5. Conclusion

The new debate on the role of social capital may parallel that on human capital to which the OECD contributed extensively in the 1960s.

In the 1960s, the OECD made a large contribution to the establishment and recognition of the concept of human capital in economics. A generation later, the issue of social capital is under debate, and there remain major ambiguities in the concept, uncertainties in the research evidence and serious measurement problems. Alongside a review of the latest evidence on human capital, this report represents an attempt to advance our understanding of social capital.

The OECD might make some further contributions.

Across the world, there is a huge range of research, analysis and policy development under way on human capital, and increasingly on social capital. It will be extremely important to keep abreast of all this activity, and to share experience of both policy implications and measurement issues, so that key conclusions can be distilled. The task of the OECD will be to identify those areas where its own contributions can add value. There are three areas where this may be helpful:

- First, the OECD has played an important role in drawing together internationally comparable indicators of human capital formation, and undertaking policy analysis on the basis of such indicators. It can continue that role, and deepen it by adding analysis of the potentially complementary roles of human and social capital.

- There has been growing policy and political interest in social capital, but few clear examples where the messages of social capital research has been unequivocally applied. There remains much fluidity about the concept, and varying terminology is common. Moreover, the idea of social capital is applicable in many diverse contexts, and it is, as yet, not clear where the use of the concept will prove most fruitful. In addition, the effectiveness of different policies in promoting social capital is as yet an almost wholly unresearched field. These considerations suggest that there might be value in a high-level OECD policy workshop designed to share the experience and policy ideas of Member countries in the light of the emerging research evidence on social capital.

- Better measures of social capital are essential, and work is under way in a number of countries to develop survey instruments. One option would be for the OECD to explore the possibility of an international pooling of resources in this area – perhaps through the development of a common survey instrument, linked to the OECD's continuing work on educational indicators. For example, one possibility which might deserve exploration would be to link measurement of social *and* human capital in a survey of adult skills. Such a vehicle would, in principle, permit assessment of the joint and relative impact of social and human capital on life chances.

Ensuring continued economic growth and improving the well-being of all are major challenges for OECD societies. In a fast-changing global economy, the value of social and human capabilities in meeting these challenges is as important as ever. The task before us is to obtain a better understanding of the role of those abilities – human and social capital. Through understanding we can make better use of human skills and devise new ways of working together to increase the well-being of all – leaving future generations at least as many opportunities as we have had.

Attention to human and social capital will help to sustain the well-being of future generations.

Notes

1. See OECD (2001, Chapter 4), for a discussion of the problem of pinning down the new skills required by the knowledge economy.

2. Epstein (1995) presents a vision of how a partnership between schools, families and communities might work: he argues that schools would become more like families in accepting all children and their families, and families would be more like schools through their promotion of a learning climate.

3. Examples of such electronic networks might include area-based bulletin boards providing information exchanges on job openings, offers of voluntary care, etc.

4. The evidence on the impact of social ties and quality of personal relations reviewed in Section 3.7 above is relevant.

Appendix A
SOME MEASURES OF WELL-BEING

Surveys of public attitudes and quality of life in various OECD countries, particularly the World Values Study, suggest that overall well-being is, increasingly, lagging behind growth in GDP. The implication is that in the developed world diminishing returns to economic growth may have set in (Inglehart, 2000; Eckersley, 1998). One implication is that more attention needs to be paid to the quality of economic growth, taking account of any other changes in the physical or social environment which are linked to economic growth, and affect well-being.

GDP and other national accounting based measures (including "green" GDP and "genuine savings" measures) are based on monetary estimates of income flows and adjustments to measurable stocks. The values of changes to stocks or the price of a given activity are determined by what consumers and societies are willing to pay. Costs and benefits which are not subject to a market cannot be readily included in this framework.

This appendix illustrates a selection of measures which have been used to compare some aspects of well-being across countries or over time. Each attempt accounts for aspects of well-being which are not accounted for in measures based on GDP or similar indicators. Some sense of the likely magnitudes of adjustments to GDP or investment can be given with reference to some of the studies reviewed below. Using data for the United States in 1965, Nordhaus and Tobin (1972) found that the value of leisure and other activities not accounted for in GDP were equivalent to approximately 100 and 50 per cent, respectively, of US GDP. Jorgenson and Fraumeni (1987) using US data for 1982 produce estimates for human capital investment at over 50% of full gross private domestic product.

While many of the approaches to measuring well-being are relatively new, the underlying rationale is not. Nordhaus and Tobin (1972) proposed a composite measure of net economic welfare by incorporating additional components into a wider measure of sustainable consumption and welfare. They made adjustments to GDP to include:

- estimates of the value of activities such as household production of childcare and other services as well as leisure;[1]
- tangible capital investment by households and government (*e.g.* consumer durables in the case of households).

Excluded elements of GDP were:

- instrumental or intermediate expenditures for "activities that are evidently not directly sources of utility themselves but are regrettably necessary inputs for activities that may yield utility" (*op. cit.*, p. 7) (*e.g.* the costs of commuting to work and public spending on police, sanitation, road maintenance, and national defence);
- capital depreciation as well as capital spending necessary to satisfy growth requirements in the future;[2]
- "the dis-amenities of urban life"[3] (*e.g.* the cost of pollution, litter, congestion and noise);
- education and health (on the grounds that they were intermediate goods whose fruits already show up in enhanced income).

Unlike Nordhaus and Tobin, Jorgenson and Fraumeni (1987) included investments in education in their measure of welfare. However, in common with Nordhaus and Tobin, they made adjustments for subsidies, household capital and consumption services as well as household production of leisure. The value of investments in education was estimated as the sum of the present values of lifetime incomes for all individuals plus the imputed value of forgone income for those in study.[4] No deductions were made for the cost of education or child-rearing. By contrast, Kendrick (1976) included estimates of the cost of education, training costs borne by employers, informal learning (from libraries, museums and print media) and the value of spending on research and development.

Most measures are composite and partially non-monetary indices. Others involve monetary-based estimates of various social trends or outcomes and their integration into a national accounting framework either directly or through satellite accounts. Examples of summary indices of well-being used include:

- The *Genuine Progress Indicator* (GPI) is a monetary-based measure of well-being using data going back to 1950.[5] It broadens the conventional accounting framework to include the economic contributions of families and communities, and of the natural habitat, along with conventionally measured economic production.
- The United Nations' *Human Development Index* (UNHDI) measures the overall achievements in a country on three basic dimensions of human development – longevity, knowledge and economic resources. It is measured by life expectancy, educational attainment (adult literacy and combined primary, secondary and tertiary enrolment) and adjusted per capita income in constant purchasing power parity (UNDP, 1990, 2000).

- An Index of Social Health (ISH) has been created in Canada based on the Fordham index of social health.[6] It is an index created from a set of socio-economic indicators, which measures progress against past performance for a specific country.[7]

- The Index of Sustainable Economic Welfare (ISEW) measures various activities which contribute to the quality of life.[8] Air pollution caused by economic activity is subtracted and the value of unpaid household labour is included. It also covers areas such as income inequality, other environmental damage, and depletion of environmental assets. The ISEW has now been calculated for the United Kingdom, Germany, Austria, Sweden, the Netherlands and Italy, as well as the United States.

The Index of Economic Well-being was developed by Osberg (1985) and further explained and illustrated in Osberg (2001) with data for the United States, the United Kingdom, Canada, Australia, Norway and Sweden for 1980-1996.[9] Osberg believes that elements omitted from consideration in GDP accounting may be especially relevant to social capital. The measure is based on four components:

- Effective per capita *consumption* flows, which includes consumption of marketed goods and services, of unmarketed goods and services, changes in life span and in leisure (market consumption per capita; government spending per capita; variation in work hours).

- Net societal *accumulation* of stocks of productive resources, including net accumulation of tangible capital and housing stocks per capita and net accumulation of human capital (expenditure per year on education applied to the total adult population) and R&D per capita, less net change in level of foreign indebtedness and social cost of environmental degradation.

- *Income distribution*, as indicated by the Gini index of inequality (income inequality after taxes), and depth and incidence of poverty.

- *Economic security* from unemployment, ill health, single parent poverty and poverty in old age.

The components of the index are presented in Figure A.1. Different weights, based on the values and judgements of the user, can be used to combine the four main components of average consumption, intergenerational bequest, inequality/poverty and insecurity. A key dimension in this index is to give an explicit weight to distributive issues both with respect to allocations to current and to future aggregate consumption and to the allocation of income and economic opportunities across different sub-groups in the current period. Since the four main components are separately identified, it is easy to conduct sensitivity analyses of the impact on perceived overall trends of different weighting of these components. The charts in Figure A.2 present results based on both the "standard" and "alternative" weighting for five countries: Australia, Canada, Sweden, the United Kingdom and the United States.

The results produced by this approach shows that in every country considered, growth in GDP per capita exceeds growth in economic well-being, although to different degrees in different countries. For all countries, adverse trends in inequality/poverty and insecurity measures meant that economic well-being tended to lag behind GDP growth. In the United States, GDP per capita increased by approximately 30% over the 1980 to 1997 period, but the index of economic well-being was almost constant, with an increase of only 4% over the period. In the United Kingdom, increases in per capita GDP were even larger (40%), but the IEW declined by almost 10%. Osberg notes that these results reflect the marked increases in economic inequality over this period. An additional factor in the case of the United States is the substantial increases in working hours. He reports that the decline in the IEW for the United Kingdom and Sweden is sensitive to the relative weighting of current consumption compared to distribution and insecurity. In the case of Australia and Canada where dependence on raw materials production is greater, there is greater fluctuation in GDP per capita than in the value of the IEW. Alternative weightings for economic insecurity and inequality do not make any major difference to the value of IEW for Canada.

Any attempt to summarise well-being in complex and increasingly diverse societies "inevitably requires a series of ethical and statistical judgements" (Osberg, 2001). The various approaches discussed above represent important initiatives to arrive at better measures but each is limited to a greater or lesser extent by:

- the selection of relevant indicators or components from the wider list of issues that need to enter into a full index of welfare;

- the weighting of the various components and indicators;

- the interpretation of quantitative trends in these components *vis-à-vis* trends in GDP which are less bounded as in the case of components such as unemployment.

Adding together a variety of indicators with arbitrary weighting and scaling can lead to endless disagreement over the weighting of the distinct components of well-being. Readers will draw their own conclusions as to whether any of these approaches represents an imperfect, but preferable alternative to GDP. A key challenge is to decide whether no summary measure at all of other aspects of well-being is better than a partial measure.

Figure A.1. **Illustration of the Osberg Index**

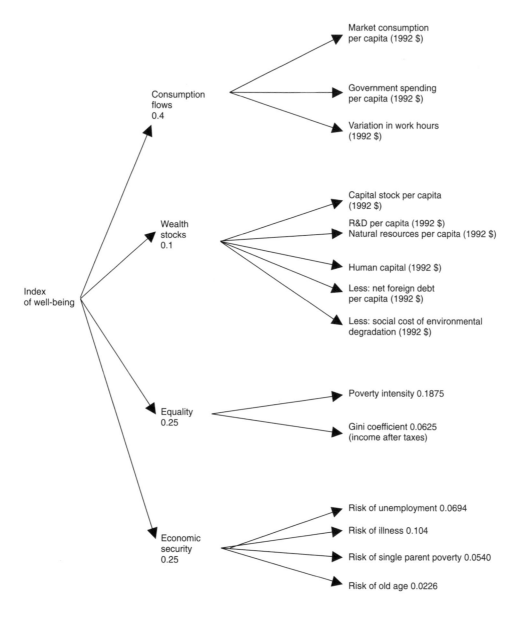

Source: Osberg (2001).

Figure A.2. **International comparisons of trends in economic well-being**

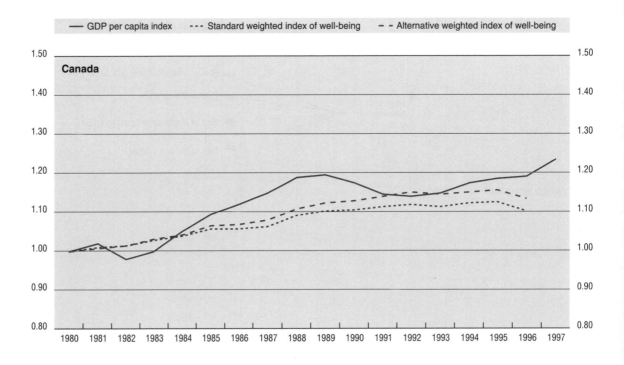

Source: Osberg (2001), Part A.

Source: Osberg (2001), Part A.

Figure A.2. **International comparisons of trends in economic well-being** *(cont.)*

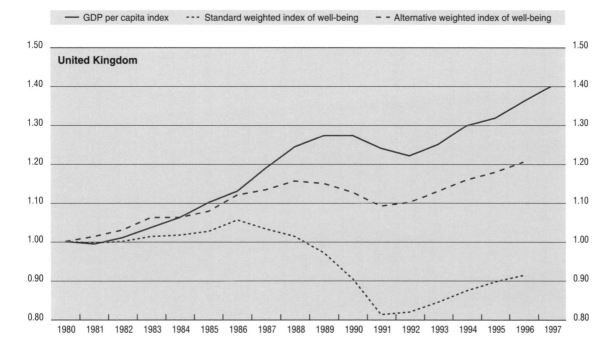

Source: Osberg (2001), Part A.

Source: Osberg (2001), Part A.

Figure A.2. **International comparisons of trends in economic well-being** *(cont.)*

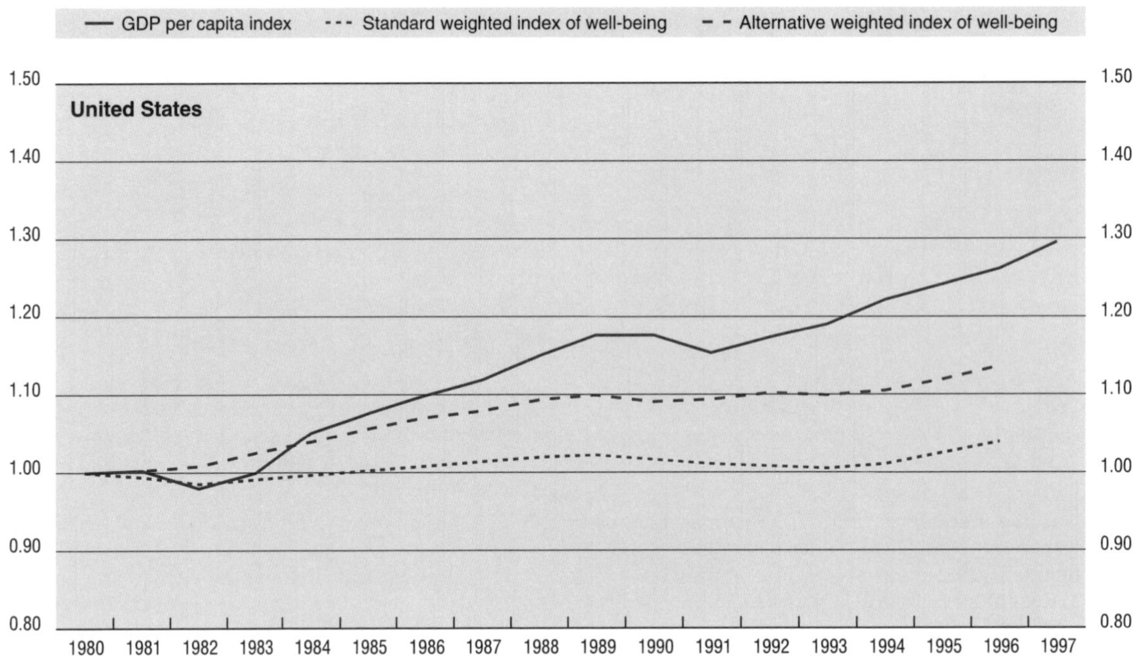

———— GDP per capita index   - - - Standard weighted index of well-being   – – Alternative weighted index of well-being

United States

Source: Osberg (2001), Part A.

Notes

1. The value of leisure was estimated by multiplying the estimated number of hours of leisure in the population aged 14 and over by wage rates (reflecting the opportunity cost of leisure).

2. That portion of capital investment required to maintain a constant capital-output ratio with consumption increasing at a rate consistent with population growth and technological progress is excluded from the measure of economic well-being.

3. No adjustments were made for environmental degradation due to lack of data.

4. The imputed value of forgone income for those in study is the difference between projected earnings of those with schooling and those without.

5. The Genuine Progress Indicator includes the following: Personal consumption; Personal consumption adjusted for income inequality; Value of housework and parenting; Net foreign lending or borrowing; Services of household capital; Services of highways and streets; Cost of underemployment; Value of volunteer work; Net capital investment; Depletion of non-renewable resources; Cost of family breakdown; Long-term environmental damage; Cost of air pollution; Cost of consumer durables; Cost of water pollution; Cost of commuting; Cost of crime; Loss of wetlands; Cost of noise and ozone pollution; Cost of household pollution abatement; Loss of leisure time.

6. Also see: Index of Social Health (1995), Monitoring the Social Well-Being of the Nation, Fordham Institute for Innovation in Social Policy, Tarrytown, N.Y.

7. The Index of Social Health (Brink and Zeesman, 1997) includes the following components: Infant mortality; Child abuse; Child poverty; Teen suicide; Drug abuse; High school drop-outs; Unemployment; Average weekly earnings; Poverty among those 65 and over; Out-of-pocket health expenditures for persons 65 and over; Highway deaths related to alcohol; Homicides; Persons receiving social assistance; Gap between rich and poor; Access to affordable housing.

8. Some of the components of the ISEW include: Consumer expenditure; Income inequality; Services from domestic labour and consumer durables; Services from streets and highways; Public expenditure on health and education; Costs of commuting; Costs of personal pollution control; Costs of automobile accidents; Costs of water, air and noise pollution; Loss of natural habitats; Loss of farmlands; Depletion of non-renewable resources; Costs of climate change and ozone depletion; Gross domestic product (see: Friends of the Earth website: *www.foe.org.uk/campaigns/sustainable_development/progress*).

9. Osberg also provides data for 8 other OECD Member countries although in some cases the underlying data are less complete (refer to Osberg, 2001).

Appendix B

SOME TRENDS IN THE SOCIAL AND ECONOMIC ENVIRONMENTS

Figure B.1. **Real gross domestic product per capita, in constant prices,
average based on selected OECD countries, 1966-99**

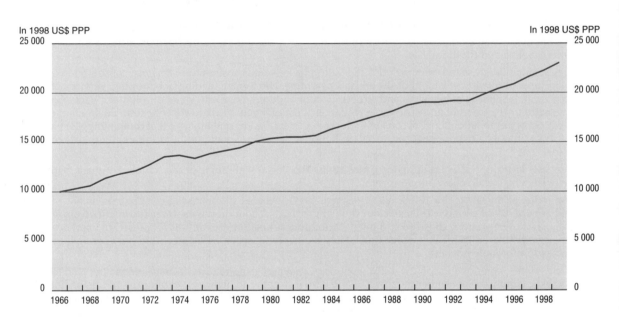

Selected countries include: Australia, Austria, Belgium, Canada, Denmark, Finland, France, Germany, Greece, Iceland, Ireland, Italy, Japan, Luxembourg, Netherlands, New Zealand, Norway, Portugal, Spain, Sweden, Switzerland, United Kingdom, United States.
Source: OECD. Real GDP deflated using 1998 US dollar. Based on Purchasing Power Parity.

Figure B.2. **Trends in income inequality for the entire population, selected OECD countries, mid-1980s and mid-1990s**

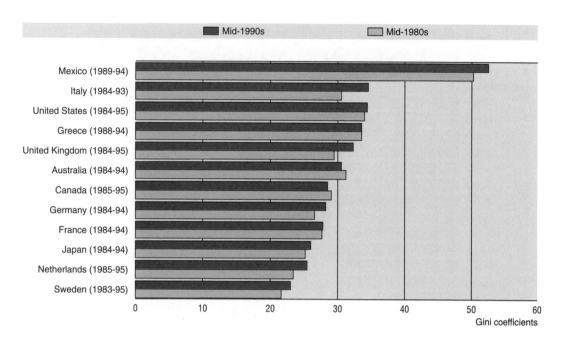

Note: Based on disposable income. Equivalence scale elasticity = 0.5.
Source: OECD (1999), "Trends in Income Distribution and Poverty in the OECD Area", document, Table 2.2.

Figure B.3. **Percentage of children living in relative poverty, selected OECD countries, 1990s**

% living in household below 50% of median income

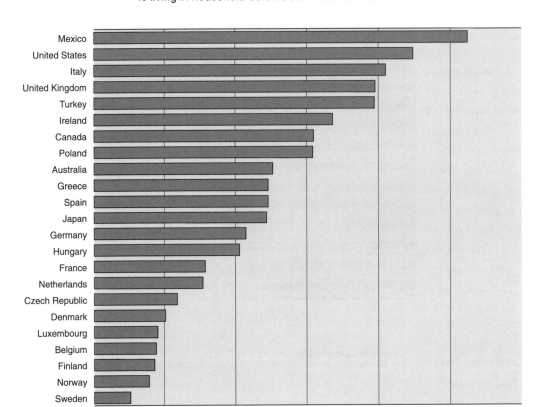

Note: Percentage of children living in relative poverty is defined as the percentage living in households below 50 per cent medium income thresh-
        old. The poverty rates refer to the following years: 1990 (Spain), 1992 (Belgium, Denmark and Japan), 1994 (Canada, France, Germany,
        Greece, Hungary, Luxembourg, Mexico, Netherlands, Turkey), 1995 (Finland, Italy, Norway, Poland, Sweden, United Kingdom), 1996 (Czech
        Republic), 1996-97 (Australia) and 1997 (Ireland, United States).
Source: UNICEF (2000), "A league table of child poverty in rich nations", *Innocenti Report Card No. 1,* UNICEF Innocenti Research Centre,
        Florence.

Figure B.4. **Unemployment rates, 25-54 year-olds and 15-24 year-olds, selected OECD countries, 1975-99**

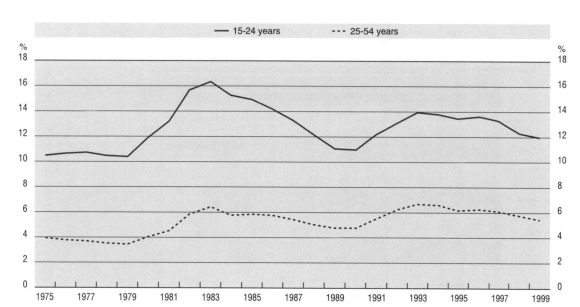

Selected countries include: Australia, Canada, Finland, France, Germany, Japan, Netherlands, Norway, Portugal, Spain, Sweden, United States.

Source: OECD (2000) based on labour force surveys. The average unemployment rates is defined as the percentage of unemployed divided by the total labour force.

Figure B.5. **Age/dependency ratios, OECD countries, 1950-2050**

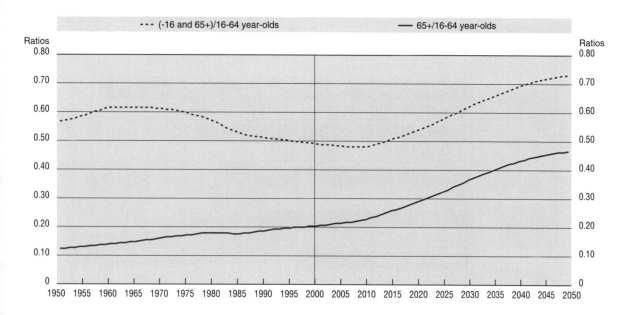

Dependency ratios: The upper line expresses the proportion of the population aged under 16 and over 65 as a percentage of the working population. The lower line shows the proportion of the population aged over 65 as a percentage of the working population.

Source: OECD (1999), *A Caring World: The New Social Policy Agenda;* United Nations (1998 revision), *World Population Prospects,* 1950-2050, medium variant.

Figure B.6. **Percentage of the population 25-64 years of age in OECD countries with completed upper secondary education or higher, 1950-98**

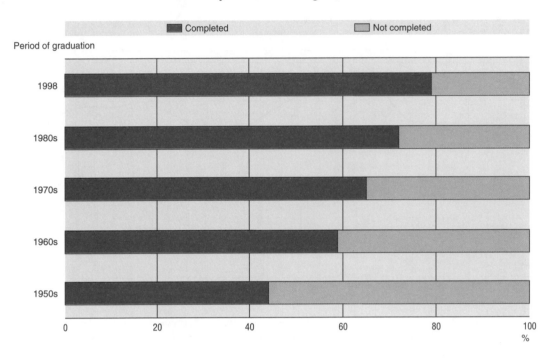

Source: OECD (2000), *Education at a Glance – OECD Indicators,* Tables C2.2, C4.2

Figure B.7. **Incidence of lone-parenting, selected OECD countries, comparison between the 1980s and 1990s**

% of households with children and one adult

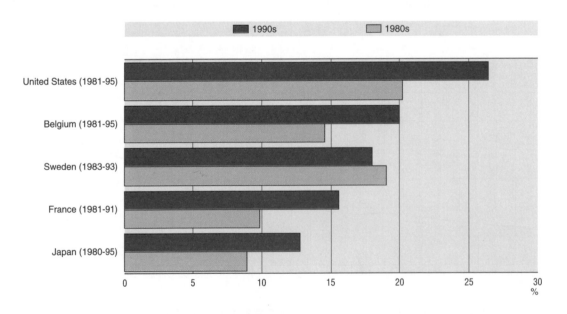

Note: Survey years in brackets.
Source: OECD based on Eurostats Demographics, 1996. Lone-parenting is defined as the percentage of households with children with one adult. The incidence is defined as the number of lone-parent families as a percentage of all families with dependent children.

Figure B.8. **Differences in earnings between men and women, 25-64 year-olds (for full-time workers), 1980s to 1990s**

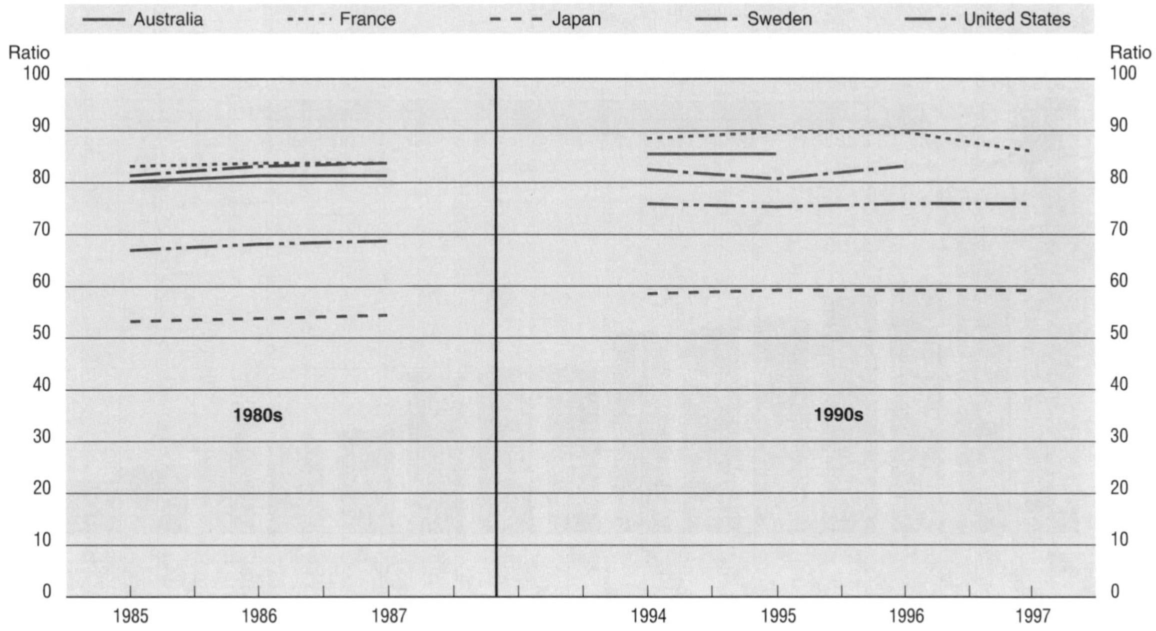

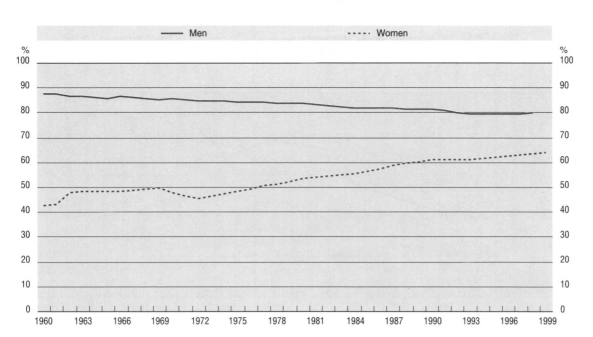

Source: OECD Structure of Earnings Database, see Keese and Puymoyen (forthcoming).

Figure B.9. **Average labour force participation rates for men and women aged 15-64, selected OECD countries, 1960-99**

Source: OECD based on labour force surveys. Average based on Australia, Canada, Finland, France, Germany, Italy, Japan, Netherlands, Norway, Portugal, Spain, Sweden, United States.

Figure B.10. **Arrivals of foreigners into OECD countries, 1999**

Per 1 000 inhabitants

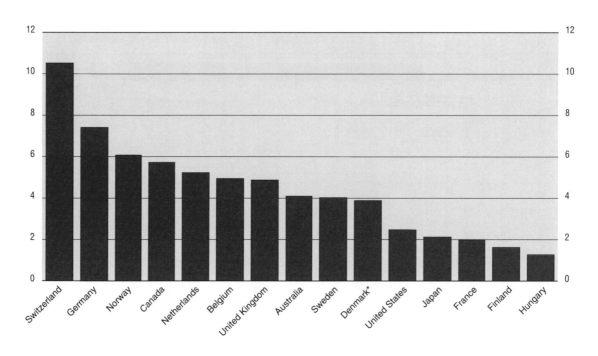

*Data for Denmark refers to 1998.

Source: OECD International Migration Database; ISTAT (1999), Annual Report.

Figure B.11. **Number of acute drug-related deaths recorded in the European Union
per million people, 1986-97**

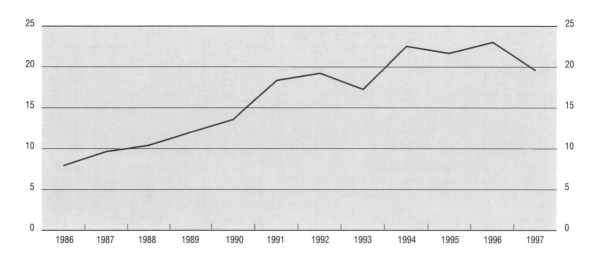

Includes: Denmark, France, Germany, Greece, Ireland, Italy, Luxembourg, Netherlands, Portugal, Spain, Sweden and United Kingdom.

Source: European Minister Conference for Drugs and Drug Addiction; UNDCP Redbook (2000), *Global Illicit Drug Trends;* UN demographic projections (1998 revisions).

Figure B.12. **Criminal victimisation rates, 1980s and 1990s**

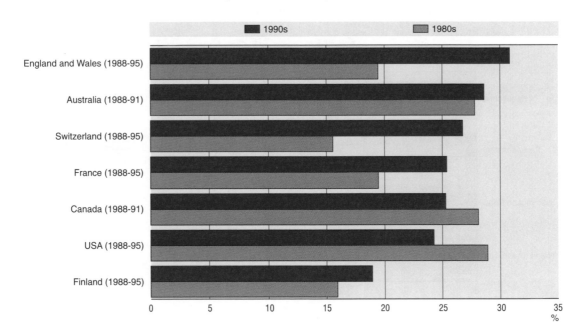

Note: Percentage of the population victimised in one year. Survey year in bracket.
Source: 1996 International Crime Victims Survey.

Figure B.13. **Average life expectancy at birth, selected OECD countries, 1960-98**

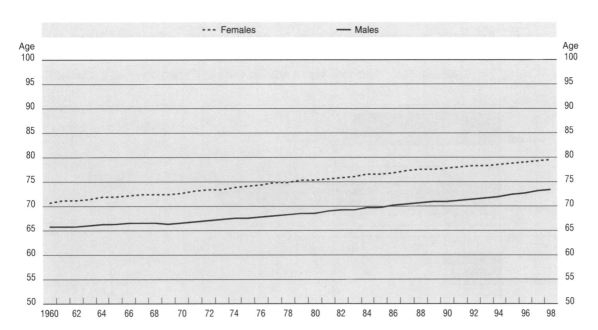

Includes: Australia, Austria, Belgium, Czech Republic, France, Germany, Hungary, Japan, Mexico, Netherlands, New Zealand, Norway, Poland, Sweden, Turkey, United States.
Source: OECD (2000), *OECD Health Data.*

Figure B.14. **Recent trend in life-satisfaction in the European Union, 12 selected countries, 1973, 1983 and 1997**

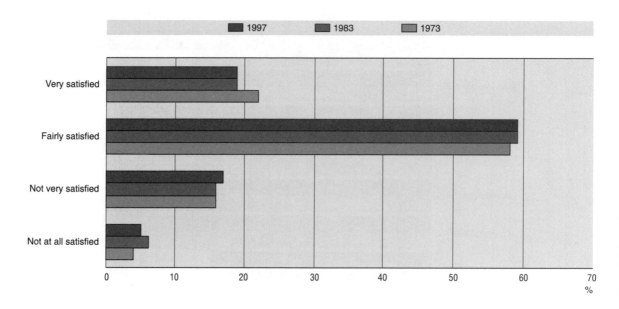

Note: Countries weighted by their relative sizes. Includes: France, Belgium, Netherlands, West Germany, Italy, Luxembourg, Denmark, Ireland, United Kingdom, Greece, Spain, Portugal.

Source: Eurobarometers cumulative file (ICPSR #9361) for 1973 and 1983 and Eurobarometer #47.1 (ICPSR #2089) for April 1997 cited in Blanchflower and Oswald (2000).

Figure B.15. **Proportion of people giving different happiness answers in the United States, 1972-98**

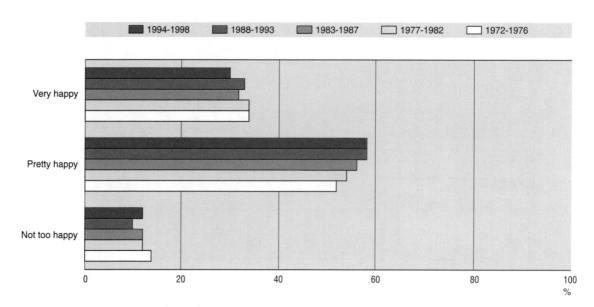

Source: US General Social Surveys cited in Blanchflower and Oswald (2000).

Figure B.16. **Suicide rate in selected OECD countries, 1950-97**

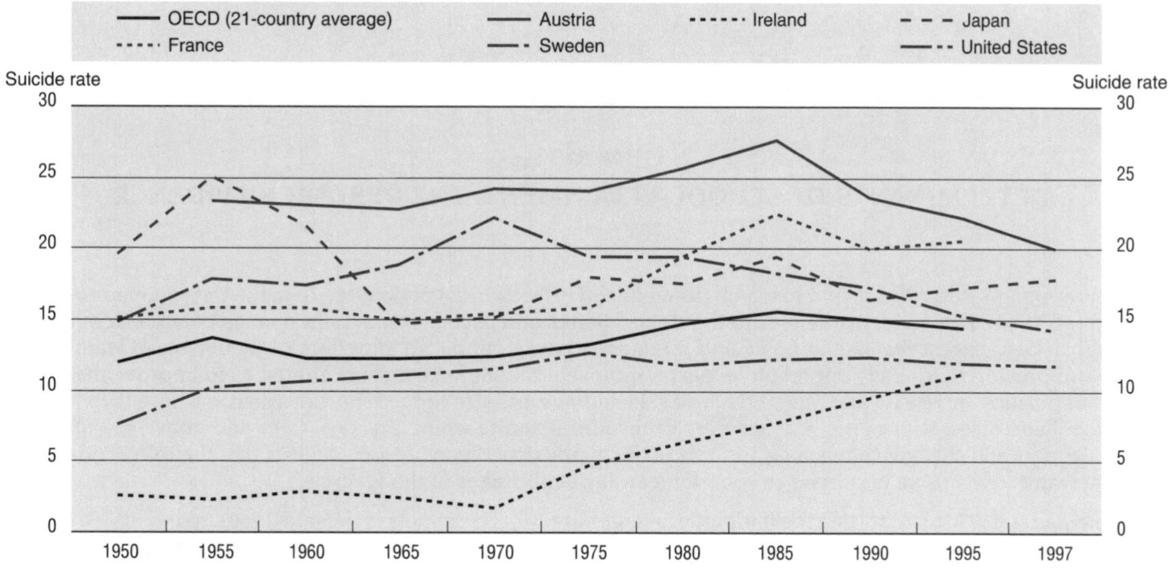

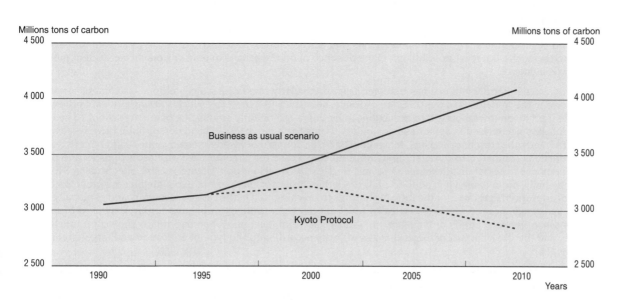

Note: 21-country average includes: Australia, Austria, Belgium, Greece, Iceland, Ireland, Italy, Japan, France, Canada, Finland, Denmark,
Luxembourg, Netherlands, New Zealand, Poland, Portugal, Spain, Sweden, Switzerland, United States.
Source: World Health Organisation.

Figure B.17. **GHG emissions in OECD countries under alternative scenarios, 1990-2010**

Note: The "Kyoto Protocol" trend line is based on the 1997 Kyoto Protocol in which industrial countries have committed themselves to differentiated
reductions of greenhouse gas emissions from 1990 levels over the period 2008-2012. The "Business as usual" trend line is a projection
based on present conditions remaining constant in the future.
Source: OECD. Projections for GHG emissions based on the OECD GREEN model.

89

Appendix C

DETERMINANTS OF SCHOOL ATTAINMENT: THE RESEARCH EVIDENCE

This appendix describes recent research (summarised in Section 2.4 of Chapter 2) on the determinants of school attainment. Most of the evidence relates to the United States and covers only a limited range of learning outcomes. However it does suggest that family, home and community backgrounds are important determinants of learning outcomes and provide potentially important levers to improve attainment, alongside strategies to improve the quality of teacher practice. Increased and targeted funding, including class size reductions, can also contribute to better performance if combined with better management of resources and teaching practice. Over and above the impact of material inputs and changes in teaching and instructional practice, the evidence suggests that the role of norms and social networks remains an important support for learning at all stages of the lifecycle.

Coleman *et al.* (1966), reporting the findings of a large survey of US schools in the mid-1960s, found little evidence that material inputs and class sizes were related to school attainment. (More recent evidence has pointed to more positive results, as well as shortcomings in the state of current and past research.) Coleman found that material school inputs affect pupil achievement only slightly, especially relative to family background. However, these results are very much conditional on the range of outcomes being assessed as well as the level of economic and social development of the societies under examination. Some learning outcomes such as those related to mathematical or scientific ability are more closely related to the impact of the school. Inter-personal and especially intra-personal skills, are more likely to be closely related to family, social and home background and affected to a lesser extent by school. A further difficulty in separating home from school effects is the fact that, for OECD countries, it is rarely possible to observe the results following from students not attending school. On the other hand, Fuller and Clarke (1994) raise the possibility that school effects may be over-stated if family and social background proxy measures are inadequate or poorly specified.

The evidence for a positive impact of class size reduction on student learning outcomes is mixed. Hanushek (1998) reviewed almost 300 different estimates of the effect of altering class size on achievement and argued that there is no indication that general reductions in class size are associated with any average improvement in student achievement. Out of 277 studies on the impact of pupil-teacher ratios reviewed by Hanushek, only 15% showed a positive and statistically significant impact on student performance, compared to 13 (just under 5%) that showed a negative and significant link. The evidence suggests that across-the-board reductions in class size will not necessarily yield better results – at least possibly not in the absence of other changes in teaching practices, student motivation and home influence.

On the other hand, evidence has emerged from particularly one large-scale "random-assignment" experiment conducted in the mid-1980s in the US State of Tennessee (the STAR project[1]) which showed modest improvements in student achievement for class size reductions in kindergarten or early grades of elementary school.[2] The positive impact of class size reduction at more senior grades seems to be much less, if at all perceptible. However, using data from STAR and other research findings, Mosteller (1995) has found that disadvantaged students do benefit from class size reductions compared to other students, thus making a case for targeted class-size reductions as one possible policy response to social disadvantage. Nye and Hedges (2000) also report large class size effects using STAR data. More generally, more research is needed on the relative impact of class size in explaining learning outcomes at all levels of education. Class size (or the ratio of students to teaching staff in the case of secondary and especially tertiary levels) varies significantly within countries by level of education (primary through to tertiary), by field of study, by type of school (special needs or mainstream) and by nature of location (urban and rural). The scope for class size changes and the likely impact of these changes will vary according to the type of education and target group under consideration.

The evidence reveals wide variation in outcomes within and across schools, as well as variations in the effectiveness of teaching practice within schools. Within schools, much of the variation in rates of learning between one grade and the next appears to depend on variations in teacher quality (Hanushek, Kain and Rivkin, 1998). Hanushek (1992) shows that the differences in student achievement with a strong versus a weak teacher can be more than 1½ grade levels of achievement within a single school year. Individual teachers differ systematically in how quickly their students learn (Murnane, 1975), even after controlling for student traits. Moreover, variations in teacher quality have been found by Rivkin, Hanushek and Kain (1998) to be more significant within schools than between schools in a district or region. Similarly, follow-up studies of graduates indicate varying labour market performance of students related to the quality of school attended (Betts, 1995) and Grogger (1996).

Other research has examined the impact of competition between schools on attainment – either through greater parental choice in a locality or through the use of voucher-type schemes where individuals buy education where they want with a publicly funded credit voucher. The impact of voucher programmes in the United States is still a hotly debated issue and the research on outcomes is still unclear. Hoxby (1994) suggests that the presence of private schools in an area appears to improve the efficiency of nearby public schools that must compete for students. Shleifer (1998) shows that private ownership of schools combined with choice and competition provides strong incentives for cost reduction and improved educational performance. However, a key concern is the equity implications of changes in competition and use of parental choice in the context of unequal opportunities and endowments of financial and social capital. Whether such innovations in the United States and elsewhere raise quality while not affecting equity remains to be seen. Furthermore, studies of various types of contractual arrangements including the performance of private and public schools are constrained by the lack of suitable controls and confounding factors.[3]

There is some cross-country evidence that the existence of central examinations as well as centralised control mechanisms with respect to standards and budgets at national or regional level can help to improve school performance[4] (Wossmann, 2000 and Bishop, 1999). Also, effective delegation of decision-making to schools or local levels of government, especially in certain areas of responsibility such as personnel policy and recruitment as well as purchase of educational material may help to improve school performance (Wossmann, 2000).[5]

Evidence from various studies covering a large range of countries (and summarised in Fuller and Clarke, 1994) suggests that availability of textbooks and supplementary reading materials as well as school library facilities have a significant impact on student achievement, especially at primary level. However, frequency and type of use made of these facilities is likely to be more crucial than the mere presence of a library in the school.

Empirical analysis of peer effects on student achievement has been limited, and what exists has been open to question because of the difficulties of identifying peer effects per se. Hanushek, Kain, Markman and Rivkin (2000) examined elementary level school achievement (in tests of mathematics and science) in the US State of Texas and showed that the achievement level and racial composition of peers has a direct influence on achievement.[6] All students appeared to benefit from having higher-achieving school peers, although the effect was found to be small.

As discussed in Chapter 2, above the quality and amount of time parents spend with their children is crucial. What parents do seems to be more important than their socio-economic status. For example, one study found that the effects of parents' engagement at home outweighed the effects associated with volunteering at school or being involved in school governance (Ho Sui-Chu and Willms, 1996). They also found that measures of parental involvement explained more than social background – reinforcing the point that the effect of social background can be considerably mitigated by differences in parental involvement and behaviour. Carlson (1999) found, using US longitudinal data, that active involvement by biological fathers, including biological fathers not living with their children, in the lives of their children can have a range of favourable impacts on adolescent behavioural outcomes, including school attendance, over and above the effect of family structure.

Some studies have focussed on the extent and quality of networks involving educators, parents and local communities. Coleman used as examples of social capital networks around schools the efforts and time invested by parents in developing strong relationships with their children, their children's teachers, their children's friends, parents of their children's friends and other adults significant in their children's lives. Mutual trust among the various individuals in such networks makes for a climate of support, surveillance and social influence. Parents are potentially more involved and better informed about their children's friends, activities and scholarly progress. A study by Coleman and Hoffer of religious, private and public schools in the US found that religious based schools had significantly lower drop out rates than non-religious private and public schools (Coleman and Hoffer, 1987). Coleman and Hoffer argued that these schools tended to perform better not only because of the existence of religious norms and precepts favourable to learning and good teaching practice, but also because of "social closure" in which parents of students are connected through school as well as wider community networks. As communities of learning, schools with higher levels of "relational trust" performed better even after accounting for various other factors including teacher background and student characteristics (Bryk, Lee and Holland, 1993, p. 314).

In the case of early childhood education and care outside the home, partnerships between providers of care and families can enhance not only children's development but also parental skills and self-esteem (Powell, 1989). Participation in effective early childhood development can also stimulate social capital networks through, for example, organisation of learning activities, operation of programmes and decision-making involving parents, carers and other staff. Furthermore, as in primary and secondary level education, early childhood education and care can generate social support networks and strong ties with other families.

Evidence on the impact of social capital on education in the United States is reviewed by Putnam (2000a). He finds a strong and significant correlation between measures of social capital at the aggregate State level and quality of learning outcomes using Standard Aptitude Test scores (SAT).[7] Putnam (2000a, pp. 299-230) reports a strong effect of state-level social capital on individual attainment. This result was achieved after controlling for a wide range of potentially confounding variables, including race, level of income, and income inequality, levels of educational completion in the adult population, poverty rates, educational spending, teachers' salaries, class size, family structure, and religious affiliation, as well as the size of the private-school sector. However even allowing for considerable controls for income and other factors, there may be other unobserved factors correlated with the proxy measures of social capital used and learning outcomes. These findings suggest that:

- higher levels of social interaction appear to have a strong positive impact on learning;
- levels of trust and informal socialising seemed to be more significant than levels of organisational membership and related measures; and
- compared to traditional policy levers such as reductions in average class size, the likely leverage of social capital seems to be greater in raising achievement scores.

Henderson and Berla (1994) conclude on the basis of a review of a large number of studies that "… the evidence is now beyond dispute. When schools work together with families to support learning, children tend to succeed not just in school, but throughout life… When parents are involved in their children's education at home, their children do better in school. When parents are involved at school, their children go further in school, and the schools they go to are better" (Coleman and Hoffer, 1987). The potential for school, community and family partnerships to support learning is especially relevant for families from disadvantaged areas and backgrounds where they can be at a treble disadvantage of poor access to income and employment as well as social networks.

Notes

1. STAR refers to the Tennessee Student-Teacher Achievement Ratio experiment.

2. For a review of the STAR project findings, see Hanushek, 1998. The STAR project used a specially designed random experiment to assign children to different size classes in kindergarten through to third grade of primary school.

3. As in other areas of the social sciences, it is not easy to entirely randomise studies since statistical controls are limited to the samples used which are drawn from a non-random environment and where group and individual selection bias is difficult to remove entirely.

4. Although the impact appears to be stronger in mathematics than in science. See Wossmann, 2000.

5. The results in relation to school autonomy and the existence of central examinations and standards hold up both at the micro level using data from the Third International Mathematics and Science Survey (TIMSS) as well as at the macro level using country averages for 39 countries participating in TIMSS.

6. The study uses various statistical methods to separate peer effects from school, community and other effects.

7. The composite measure used by Putnam is made up of indicators of: *i*) intensity of involvement in community, organisational life; *ii*) public engagement (*e.g.* voting); *iii*) community volunteering; *iv*) informal sociability (*e.g.* visiting friends); and *v*) reported levels of trust.

Appendix D

THE IMPACT OF HUMAN CAPITAL ON ECONOMIC GROWTH: SOME MAJOR STUDIES

Table D.1. **The impact of education in cross-country regression analysis: some major studies**

Author(s)	Sample(s)	Data	Education variable(s)	Impact of education variable(s)
OECD (2001) (Bassanini and Scarpetta)	21 OECD countries	OECD data on education attainment and the revised Barro-Lee (1996) dataset based on the work of de la Fuente and Domenech (2000).	Educational attainment	Find that the coefficients on human capital suggest relatively high returns to education: one extra year of average education (corresponding to a rise in human capital by about 10 per cent) would lead to an average increase in steady-state output per capita by about 4-7 per cent.
Barro (2001)	Developed and developing countries (81 countries with a sub-sample of 23 OECD countries)	Heston and Summers (1991); Barro-Lee (2000)	Educational attainment Test scores – for science, mathematics, and reading	Positive only for developing countries (only for men). Little or no significant impact of education in sample comprising high-income countries.
De la Fuente and Domenech (2000)	21 OECD countries	OECD data on education attainment and the revised Barro-Lee (1996) dataset.	Educational attainment	Their work reveals many errors and inconsistencies in the "Barro-Lee" educational attainment dataset (1996). Using their revised Barro-Lee dataset, they find a strongly significant coefficient for human capital in level and growth equations.
Hanushek and Kimko (2000)	Developed and developing countries (31 countries)	Barro-Lee (1997) complemented by series of international tests in maths and science	Measures of labour force quality based on student cognitive performance on various international tests of academic achievement in mathematics and science.	Conclude that labour force quality has a consistent, stable, and strong relationship with economic growth. At the same time, the simple estimates of cross-country growth relationships appear to overstate the causal impact of quality.
Krueger and Lindahl (1999)	Developed and developing countries, as well as a subset of OECD countries.	Heston and Summers (1991); Barro-Lee (1993).	Educational attainment	Believe that the failure to find a significant human capital/growth relationship lies in measurement errors in education data or inconsistencies in the way data on human capital are collected and compared. To prove their case, they examine the correlation between two different measures of the change in average years of schooling that have been used in the literature. They find that the correlation is low enough to suggest that a substantial component of the measured change in educational attainment is uninformative noise.
Pritchett (1999)	Developed and developing countries	Barro-Lee (1993) and Nehru, Swanson and Dubey (1995)	Enrolment rates and educational attainment	Finds that increases in educational enrolment or attainment have had no significant positive impact on the rate of growth of productivity or economic growth. Arrives at essentially the same conclusion when using the growth rate of total factor productivity in a non-regression growth accounting framework.
Temple (1999b)	Developed and developing countries	Benhabib and Spiegel (1994)	Educational attainment	Noted that a strong relation can be discerned when some influential outliers are eliminated.
Barro and Lee (1997)	Developed and developing countries (around 100 countries)	Heston and Summers (1991); Barro-Lee (1997)	Educational attainment	An extra year of male upper-level schooling is estimated to raise the growth rate by 1.2 percentage point per year. Secondary and higher education as determinant of economic growth (for male only).

Table D.1. **The impact of education in cross-country regression analysis: some major studies** (*cont.*)

Author(s)	Sample(s)	Data	Education variable(s)	Impact of education variable(s)
Gemmell (1996)	Developed and developing countries (98 countries)	Mankiw, Romer and Weil's (1992) sample with sub-sample for OECD and less developed countries	Use school enrolment rates to estimate stock of initial primary, secondary and tertiary human capital.	Finds that while primary and secondary education are important for growth in developing countries, skills are important for growth in OECD countries.
Jones (1996)	Developed and developing countries	Heston and Summers (1991); Barro-Lee (1993)	Educational attainment	Finds that future workers benefit (in terms of their productivity) from the education of current workers via the resulting (current) production of new ideas.
Barro and Sala-i-Martin (1995)	Developed and developing countries	Heston and Summers (1991); Barro-Lee (1994)	Educational attainment	Find that the initial stock of human capital on economic growth matters for males: – Increases in average male secondary schooling by 0.68 year raises annual growth by 1.1 percentage point per year. – A mere 0.09 year increase in average male tertiary education raises annual growth by as much as 0.5 percentage point. Female education (both secondary and tertiary) shows a negative impact on economic growth.
Hanushek and Kim (1995)	Developed and developing countries	Barro-Lee (1993) complemented by series of international tests in maths and science	Measures of labour force quality based on student cognitive performance on various international tests of academic achievement in mathematics and science.	Find that scores on international examinations – indicators of the quality of schooling capital – matter more than years of attainment for subsequent economic growth. They find inclusion of their labour force quality variable raises the explanatory power of the model while it reduces the coefficient on school quantity. Their analysis reveals that, in one of their simpler specifications, a standard deviation increase in labour force quality increases real per capita growth rate by one per cent per year, almost the same result as a standard deviation increase in school quantity.
Jenkins (1995a)	United Kingdom	U.K. General Household Survey	Higher education	Estimates gross social returns to higher education qualification are generally greater than the micro estimates of private rates of return, which are typically around the lower end of the 26-86% range.
Jenkins (1995b)	United Kingdom, United States and Sweden	General Household Surveys	Higher education	Results show that estimated social rates of return to higher education exceed private returns in the UK, US and Sweden. Estimated social return was greater than the apparent wage premium associated with higher education in the US and Sweden.
Gittleman and Wolff (1995)	Developed and developing countries	Heston and Summers (1988) with World Bank data on education	Number of scientists and engineers per capita	Find that university enrolment rates are positively associated with labour productivity growth and that the number of scientists and engineers per capita is significant across a wide range of specifications.

97

Table D.1. **The impact of education in cross-country regression analysis: some major studies** (*cont.*)

Author(s)	Sample(s)	Data	Education variable(s)	Impact of education variable(s)
Benhabib and Spiegel (1994)	Developed and developing countries (78 countries)	Heston and Summers (1991) Human capital stock estimates by Kyriacou (1991)	Educational attainment	Find, in the large sample, that change in education is not a determinant of economic growth. But find a positive impact for the wealthiest third of the sample.
Englander and Gurney (1994)	19 OECD countries over 4 time periods between 1960 and 1990.	OECD's Analytical Data Bank (ADB)	Primary and secondary school enrolment rates	Find that enrolment rate in secondary education has contributed 0.6 per cent to annual productivity growth in OECD countries between 1960 and 1985.
Nehru and Dhareshwar (1994)	Developed and developing countries	World Bank investment data	Indices of educational attainment (derived from enrolment rates)	Human capital accumulation is three to four times as important as raw labour in explaining output growth. Total factor productivity growth between 1960 and 1987 is strongly associated with the initial level of human capital – particularly for East Asian economies.
Wolff and Gittleman (1993)	19 industrial market economies.	Heston and Summers (1988) with World Bank data on education	Enrolment rates and educational attainment	For OECD countries, only tertiary enrolment rates are significant, whilst education attainment is more significant for primary education. They note that inclusion of investment strongly affects the significance of the educational attainment variables.
Mankiw *et al.* (1992)	Testing three different samples, ranging in size from 22 to 98 countries – including a sample of 22 OECD countries	Heston and Summers (1988); UNESCO (education).	Secondary school enrolment rates	Find that the coefficient on physical investment is reduced when the human capital variable is included while the explanatory power of the model increases (close to 80 per cent of the observed cross-country income variation). However, more education will raise an economy's short-run growth rate (or permanent income level) but not its long-run growth.
Barro (1991)	Developed and developing countries (around 100 countries)	Heston and Summers (1988); United Nations data	Differences in real school resources as a crude measure of quality differences across countries	The student-teacher ratio in primary schools in 1960 had a negative relationship to economic growth. The student-teacher ratio in secondary schools was statistically insignificant with a positive sign.
Romer (1990b)	Developed and developing countries	Heston and Summers (1988); UNESCO (education)	Literacy	Finds that the initial level of literacy helps to predict the subsequent rate of investment, and indirectly, the rate of growth.

Appendix E

ARE TRUST AND CIVIC ENGAGEMENT DECLINING IN OECD COUNTRIES?

This appendix provides evidence on trust and civic engagement in respect of eight countries: the United States, the United Kingdom, the Netherlands, Sweden, Australia, Japan, France, and Germany.

United States

Putnam (2000*a* and *b*) reports significant declines in group membership and informal socialising in the United States. He uses data from various sources (including the US *General Social Survey*, the Roper Social and Political Trends Survey and the DDB Needham Life Style survey which provide a rich range of data over a number of decades). Declines in rates of membership of formal organisations have been accompanied by an even sharper fall in intensity of participation (number of meetings, willingness to assume leadership roles, etc.). This occurred in spite of rising education levels, which tend to be associated with higher civic engagement. In the mid-1970s, nearly two-thirds of Americans reported attendance at club meetings in the previous twelve months (see Figure E.1). In the late-1990s, nearly two thirds never attend.* Political, civic, religious and professional engagement have declined in the last 25 years in the United States, whether measured in terms of absolute number of members or in terms of "market share" (the proportion of a target population eligible to be members of a given organisation).

Such evidence raises a number of questions. The changes could be either temporary, or the inevitable result of changing social norms and patterns. Alternatively, the observed trends might be misleading, if other less traditional forms of social organisation have been increasing, but are not reflected in the long time series of data. For example

Figure E.1. **Club meeting attendance dwindles in the United States, 1975-1999**

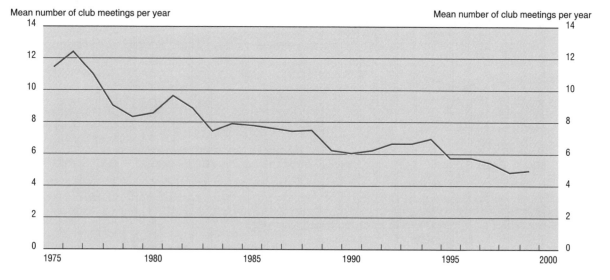

Data: DDB Needham Life Style survey archive, 1975-99.
Source: Robert Putnam, *Bowling Alone*, Figure 11, p. 61 (Simon and Schuster, 2000).

---

* Moreover, measured in terms of hours per month, the average American's investment in organisational life (apart from religious groups) fell from 3.7 hours per month in 1965 to 2.9 in 1975 to 2.3 in 1985 and 1995, Putnam (2000*a*), pp. 61-62.

new social movements such as those associated with gender, environmental, civil rights issues or "single-issue" organisations may be increasing in strength. The evidence is mixed but does tend to indicate that involvement in such groups is often less intense and sustained than in the more traditional sectors of civic association. Membership in some of these organisations rises and falls quickly and in many cases is based on "mailing lists". Informal self-help and support groups have certainly grown, but engagement appears to be more transient, short-lived and less often associated with general public interests.

Various forms of informal social connectedness (such as incidence of eating dinner together regularly with family, picnics, card-playing, having friends for dinner, visiting and eating out, etc.) have also waned over a long period of time. Time-use by individuals appears to have shifted towards themselves and immediate family and away from the wider community. In the case of sporting events, spectator attendance is up (as for visits to museums, cinemas, etc.) but active involvement in sport (or musical activity) is down.

There has also been a decline in general levels of inter-personal trust. The decline is highly age-specific with the baby boomers (those born in the period 1945-1965) and Generation-X (those born after 1965) less trusting than previous generations. Over time, levels of trust have been stable within cohorts. Grandparents are more than twice as likely to trust other people as grandchildren (50 per cent vs. 20 per cent). They vote at nearly double the rate of the most recent cohorts (80-85 per cent vs. 45-50 per cent) and are nearly twice as interested in politics (55 per cent vs. 30-35 per cent). Declining trust, political interest and activity in the USA are mainly inter-generational.

Another possible indicator of lower levels of trust or trustworthiness is the increase in the number of lawyers from 1970 onwards linked to what Putnam describes as "preventive lawyering". Putnam suggests that the stability in lawyer numbers up to 1970 in spite of profound social and economic change is indicative of specific shifts that have occurred since the late 1960s (see Figure E.2).

Figure E.2. **Demand for legal and security has increased in the United States, 1900-1997**

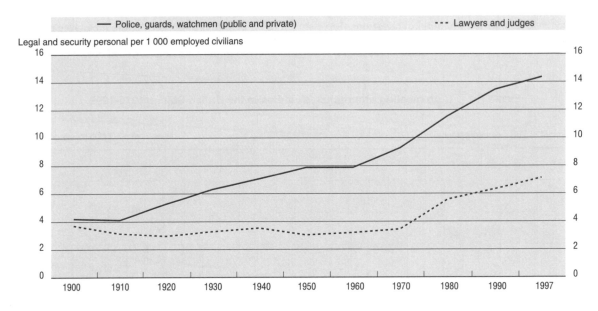

Data: 1900-70: *Historical Statistics of the United States*, Part I, D589-D592, 144; 1970-96: *Statistical Abstract of the United States* and data provided directly by the Bureau of Labor Statistics (BLS).

Source: Robert Putnam, *Bowling Alone*, Figure 42, p. 145 (Simon and Schuster, 2000).

Rates of participation in voluntary community, social and charitable activity tend to be higher among middle-aged and older people as compared to younger groups. Altruism, volunteering and philanthropy are highly correlated with each other. Giving time and money is related to communal involvement more than education, wealth, and size of community, family status and employment. In spite of decreasing civic engagement in other areas, there has been an increase in volunteering in the United States concentrated in older age-cohorts (what Putnam calls the "long civic generation" born between 1910 and 1940). The nature of volunteering has shifted towards more individual-to-individual care rather than group activity at the community level.

United Kingdom

Hall (1999) finds that most types of associational membership have increased since the 1950s. The United Kingdom shares with the United States a long tradition of civic culture with high levels of social trust, and political and civic participation (Almond and Verba, 1963). Unlike the US case, Hall finds no evidence of declining engagement over time even among the younger age-cohort (thus countering the hypothesis that inter-generational shifts are occurring which are not yet showing up in the aggregate population data). There has been some fall-off in membership of traditional women's or religious organisations. However, he does not have data to review the intensity of engagement or the quality of such engagement over time. It is possible that membership has tended to shift away from public-interest type organisations towards self-help or single-issue organisations. Also, face-to-face participation may have declined to be replaced by less formal and less sustained forms of commitment. The data do not permit an analysis of these possibilities.

Hall does, however, find evidence of an increasing gap in membership rates and in reported levels of trust between various social groups including by level of educational attainment. Trust and engagement are positively correlated with level of education and tend to be higher for the middle class than for the working class. Hall also finds that the relative importance of various groups has changed with declines in the population share of the less educated and of the working class relative to the 1950s. He suggests that educational reform and expansion coupled with changing social class structure may have bolstered levels of trust and civic engagement in the United Kingdom, sustaining overall levels of social capital. Government support for voluntary activity (social support, care of the elderly, community projects, etc.) may also have played a significant role. Rates of participation in community life increased for women. Three factors underlying this are identified: the increased participation by women in higher education, the growing participation of women in the labour force, and general changes in the social situation of women. In particular, the level of participation in community life for those with higher education (whether men or women) has increased more than for other levels of educational attainment (although participation is up for all levels). This may imply a higher marginal impact on social capital from higher education compared to the past.

Time-use survey data covering 1961 to 1984 shows no clear evidence for increased privatisation of leisure or decreased levels of socialising with others (although time spent visiting friends is down especially among full-time male workers). However levels of inter-personal trust have declined. In 1959, 56 per cent of all respondents to the UK Civic Culture Survey said they generally trust others, while the corresponding figure for 1995 was only 31 per cent (UK World Values Study). Hall also points to the possibility of important shifts in values and attitudes over time which impinge on the quality of civic engagement and trust. This seems to be part of a more general trend towards more materialistic and individualist values noted in Chapters 1 and 3. Putnam (2000b) also notes significant shifts in values and attitudes of young people compared to the same age-group 20-30 years ago. Declining levels of trust seem to affect the young more than other age-groups. The data for the UK show declining levels of trust:

- between persons (described here as generalised inter-personal trust); and
- towards institutions and public authorities.

Overall, the UK seems to be characterised by increased associational life and informal socialising coupled with declining levels of trust. Behind increasing levels of associational life, the gap between "well-connected and highly-active groups of citizens" and others whose associational life and civic engagement are very limited has grown since the 1950s. The two groups most affected are the young and the working class. It is also notable that those having experienced divorce, unemployment or relocation to a larger city are less inclined to participate or to trust, other things being equal.

Netherlands

The evidence for the Netherlands does not indicate any overall decline in social capital, but suggests some possible changes in types of engagement. De Hart and Dekker (1999) review data on membership of various types of organisations and rates of volunteering. Membership as well as intensity of engagement is increasing for most types of organisations (except for traditional women's organisations and political parties). Between 1980 and 1985, voluntary work was stable or increased although it declined among the 18-34 age-group (Dutch time budget survey). Political activism has tended to increase and voter turnout at key elections has remained stable. However, as in other European countries, engagement may have shifted towards less intensive and less committed forms. Rapidly growing interest groups include the "single-issue" social movements established around environmental, international solidarity and moral issues. While it is difficult to assess the extent of active involvement in these types of organisations, involvement could be more transient and less orientated to broader public interests than other types of civic organisations. Finally, time budget data do not point to declining levels of informal socialising or engagement.

Sweden

Rothstein (1998) reviews evidence indicating a deterioration in what he terms "organised social capital," that is, trust within and among the major labour and business organisations during a period of sustained consensus and participation of the social partners in economic and social planning. As in Britain, declining levels of trust in political institutions are found, parallel to declining levels of co-operation, consensus and trust from the late 1980s onwards. Political engagement also appears to be changing from active involvement to passive spectatorship and interest. Whereas the data show that levels of political interest are rising, fewer people are actively involved: party volunteers are older and professionalisation of politics and more intensive media involvement have tended to sideline the role of such volunteers. Professional campaigns and media activity have tended to supplant popular mobilisation, debate and study circles. As in other European countries, membership of single-issue organisations has grown in importance relative to stable, mass organisations.

Traditionally, Sweden along with other Scandinavian countries has occupied one of the top positions in international rankings of organisational engagement, volunteering and self-reported levels of general trust. Evidence from national as well as international surveys such as the World Values Study suggests that both formal and informal social organisations have, if anything, displayed increasing vitality in recent decades. Rothstein does find evidence of increasing individualism, as younger generations have turned away from traditional hierarchically organised forms of social activity. So, for example religious temperance movements and women's organisations have given way to leisure, sports, cultural, and environmental organisations. As in the case of the United Kingdom, rates of organisational membership differ among groups and are highest among the young. Membership of organisations over time is up across all age-groups and social classes, and the gap between men and women has narrowed (as in the UK). World Values Study data also point to higher levels between 1981 and 1996. The Swedish Level of Living surveys from 1968, 1981 and 1991 also support these results.

However, other studies point to lower levels of "affinity" to certain mass organisations. This may be connected in the view of Rothstein to rising discernment and lower collective or group identity. Other studies again show increasing levels of individualism and personal autonomy. Rothstein argues that this may be compatible with a more "solidaristic" individualism (by contrast with an egoistic individualism).

Australia

The evidence for Australia is more akin to that for the United States. Declining membership has been noted by Eva Cox (in Putnam, 2000b) for many long-term established voluntary groups in recent decades. For example, trade union membership and church attendance both fell significantly from the 1960s to the 1990s. Volunteering appears also to have declined, while the evidence for political involvement is not as clear-cut. Generalised inter-personal trust and trust in political institutions have clearly declined in the last 15 years. Television-watching has increased and informal socialising has decreased. In the view of Cox, declines in trust may be linked to increased anxiety about the future as well as rising inequalities. Though sports participation is up, as it appears to be elsewhere, this trend is likely to reflect individual fitness activities, rather than team sports. Some social movements such as feminist and environmentalist groups appear to have lost ground.

Japan

Inoguchi (in Putnam, 2000b) finds some evidence of rising levels of civic engagement and membership of non-governmental organisations in Japan. Membership of neighbourhood groups has not changed significantly since the mid-1980s. Involvement in voluntary caring organisations serving children, the aged, and the disadvantaged has increased substantially.

The "radius" of social trust is perhaps narrower in Japan than in Northern Europe and the United States. Inoguchi argues that trust and co-operation are stronger in smaller and more intimate circles of families, close friends and professional or work associates. Fukuyama (1995) also sees trust in Japanese society as being characterised by the development of large-scale corporations out of family firms through the medium of a "rich and complex civil society" (p. 130). Lean manufacturing in Japan is presented as the model of the "high trust workplace" where the role of the workers is to contribute their judgement to help run the production line as a whole (pp. 258-259). There seems to be evidence of a gradual increase in generalised trust, suggesting that Japan may be gradually converging toward patterns prevailing elsewhere. There is little data on levels of informal socialising.

France

Evidence considered by Worms in Putnam (2000b) indicates no decline in associational life. While some of the principal social and political organisations, especially trade unions, political parties, and the church, have experienced declining membership, membership in other types of associations has been stable. Social policies and provision may have sustained non-profit social service organisations. Two trends in recent decades are notable. First, an increase in organisations pursuing sectoral or particular group interests followed by an increase in membership of more broad-interest organisations. Second, there has been an increase in personal development associations in the form of cultural and leisure activities. Education is seen to partly account for these changes.

As in other countries, civic participation seems to have shifted towards more informal and transient affiliations. Worms argues that the shifting nature of engagement evokes a "missing link" between private sociability and the wider public interest especially in terms of linkage to public institutions. However, the difference in level of civic engagement between France and other countries remains notable. France lags behind not only the United States and Scandinavian countries but also behind Germany, Belgium, the United Kingdom, and Ireland in terms of membership, number of volunteers and donors. Worms raises the possibility that historical influences of Church and State in competing for control of civil society left little room for citizen initiative.

Germany

From depressed levels in 1945, formal participation as well as informal sociability have increased in Germany (Offe and Fuchs, 1998). This is particularly evident among the younger generation. The main exceptions were: 1) falling membership in trade unions, political parties, and churches; and 2) an apparent disengagement of younger Germans from political and social organisations during the 1990s. As in Sweden, there is evidence of a trend away from formal membership organisations toward more transient and personalistic involvement. Patterns in the distribution of social involvement among groups are quite similar to those in the United States – more associational involvement (especially of a formal sort) among the more educated and more affluent, but also among those in the labour force, the middle-aged, in smaller towns, and among men (especially in more "public" forms of activity, though with the gender gap closing over time).

REFERENCES

ABRAMOVITZ, M. and DAVID, P. (1996),
"Convergence and Deferred Catch-up: Productivity Leadership and the Waning of American Exceptionalism", in R. Landau, T. Taylor and G. Wright (eds.), *The Mosaic of Economic Growth*, Stanford University Press, Standford, CA.

ABRAMS, P. and BULMER, M. (1986),
Neighbours, Cambridge University Press, Cambridge, United Kingdom.

ACEMOGLU, D. (1996),
"A Microfoundation for Social Increasing Returns in Human Capital Accumulation", *Quarterly Journal of Economics*, Vol. 111, pp. 779-804.

ADLER, P. and KWON, S. (2000),
"Social Capital: The Good, the Bad, and the Ugly", University of Southern California.

AGHION, P. and HOWITT, P. (1998),
Endogenous Growth Theory, MIT Press, Cambridge, MA.

ALESINA, A. and RODRIK, D. (1992),
"Income Distribution and Economic Growth: A Simple Theory and Empirical Evidence", in A. Cukierman, Z. Hercowitz and L. Leiderman (eds.), *The Political Economy of Business Cycles and Growth*, MIT Press, Cambridge, MA.

ALMOND, G. and VERBA, S. (1963),
The Civic Culture: Political Attitudes and Democracy in Five Nations, Princeton University Press, Princeton.

AMATO, P. (1998),
"More than Money? Men's Contributions to their Children's Lives", in A. Booth and A. Creuter (eds.), *Men in Families: When do they get involved? What difference does it make?*, Lawrence Erlbaum, New Jersey, Chapter 13.

ANGRIST, J. and KRUEGER, A.B. (1991a),
"Does Compulsory School Attendance Affect Schooling and Earnings?", *Quarterly Journal of Economics*, Vol. 106, pp. 979-1014.

ANGRIST, J. and KRUEGER, A.B. (1991b),
"Estimating the Payoff to Schooling Using the Vietnam-Era Lottery", Princeton University Industrial Relations Section, Working Paper No. 290, August.

ARROW, K.J. (1972),
"Gifts and Exchanges," *Philosophy and Public Affairs*, No. 1, Summer.

ASHENFELTER, O. and KRUEGER, A.B. (1994),
"Estimates of the Economic Return to Schooling from a New Sample of Twins", *American Economic Review*, Vol. 84, No. 5, December, pp. 1157-1173.

AXELROD, R. (1984),
The Evolution of Cooperation, Penguin, New York.

BAKER, B. and BENJAMIN, D. (1994),
"The Performance of Immigrants in the Canadian Labor Market", *Journal of Labour Economics*, Vol. 12, No. 3.

BARBIERI, P., RUSSELL, H. and PAUGAM, S. (1999),
"Social Capital and Exits from Unemployment", Unpublished paper.

BARRO, R.J. (1991),
"Economic Growth in a Cross-section of Countries", *Quarterly Journal of Economics*, CVI, May.

BARRO, R.J. (2001),
"Education and Economic Growth", in J.F. Helliwell (ed.), *The Contribution of Human and Social Capital to Sustained Economic Growth and Well-being: International Symposium Report*, Human Resources Development Canada and OECD.

BARRO, R.J. and LEE, J.W. (1993),
"International Comparisons of Educational Attainment", NBER Working Paper No. 4349.

BARRO, R.J. and LEE, J.W. (1994),
"Data Set for a Panel of 138 Countries", Revised January, 1994.

BARRO, R.J. and LEE, J.W. (1996),
"International Measures of Schooling Years and Schooling Quality", *American Economic Review*, Papers and Proceedings 86, No. 2, pp. 218-223.

BARRO, R.J. and LEE, J.W. (1997),
"Schooling Quality in a Cross-section of Countries", NBER Working Paper No. 6198.

BARRO, R.J. and LEE, J.W. (2000),
"International Data on Educational Attainment: Updates and Implications", Center for International Development (CID), Working Paper No. 42, Harvard University, April.

BARRO, R.J. and SALA-I-MARTIN, X. (1995),
Economic Growth, McGraw-Hill, New York.

BASSANINI, A. and SCARPETTA, S. (2001),
"Links between Policy and Growth: Evidence from OECD Countries", OECD Economics Department Working Papers.

BECKER, G. (1993),
"Human Capital: A theoretical and Empirical Analysis, with Special Reference to Education", The University of Chicago Press, Chicago, Third Edition.

BEHRMAN, J.R. and STACEY, N. (eds.) (1997),
The Social Benefits of Education, The University of Michigan Press, Ann Arbor.

BENHABIB, J. and SPIEGEL, M. (1994),
"The Role of Human Capital in Economic Development: Evidence from Aggregate Cross-Country Data", *Journal of Monetary Economics*, Vol. 43, pp. 143-174.

BETTS, J. (1995),
"Does School Quality Matter? Evidence from the National Longitudinal Survey of Youth", *Review of Economics and Statistics*, May, No. 77(2), pp. 231-250.

BETTS, J. and ROEMER, J. (1998),
"Equalizing Opportunity through Educational Finance Reform", Department of Economics, University of California, San Diego.

BIBLARZ, T., RAFTERY, A. and BUCUR, A. (1997),
"Family Structure and Social Mobility", *Social Forces*, Vol. 75(4), pp. 1319-1339.

BISHOP, J. (1999),
"Are National Exit Examinations Important for Educational Efficiency?", *Swedish Economic Policy Review*, Vol. 6(2), pp. 349-398.

BLANCHFLOWER, D.G. and OSWALD, A.J. (2000),
"Well-being over Time in Britain and the USA", Working Paper No. 7487, National Bureau of Economic Research, Cambridge, MA (http://www.nber.org/papers/w7487).

BLOSSFELD, H.P. and SHAVIT, Y. (1993),
Persistent Inequality: Changing Educational Attainment in Thirteen Countries, Westview Press Inc, Colorado.

BOOTHBY, D. (1999),
"Literacy Skills, the Knowledge Content of Occupations and Occupational Mismatch", *Applied Research Branch Research Papers*, Human Resources Development Canada, August.

BORJAS, G.J. (1998),
"The Economic Progress of Immigrants", NBER Working Paper No. 6506.

BOURDIEU, P. (1979),
"Les trois états du capital culturel", *Actes de la recherche en sciences sociales*, No. 30 ("L'institution scolaire"), pp. S.3-6.

BOURDIEU, P. (1980),
"Le capital social: notes provisoires", *Actes de la recherche en sciences sociales* I, No. 31, pp. 2-3.

BOURDIEU, P. (1985),
"The Forms of Capital", in J.E. Richardson (ed.), *Handbook of Theory of Research for the Sociology of Education*, Greenwood Press, New York, pp. 241-258.

BOURDIEU, P. and PASSERON, J.C. (1970),
Reproduction in Education, Society and Culture, Sage, London.

BRINK, S. and ZEESMAN, A. (1997),
"Measuring Social Well-Being: An Index of Social Health for Canada", HRDC Working Paper, R-97-9E.

BROWN, G. and HARRIS, T. (1978),
Social Origins of Depression, Tavisock, London.

BRYK, A.S., LEE, V.E. and HOLLAND, P.B. (1993),
Catholic Schools and the Common Good, Harvard University Press, Cambridge, MA.

BURT, R.S. (1992),
Structural Holes, The Social Structure of Competition, Harvard University Press, Cambridge, MA.

BYNNER, J., MCINTOSH, S., VIGNOLES, A., DEARDEN, L., REED, H. and VAN REENEN, J. (2001),
Wider Benefits of Learning Improving Adult Basic Skills: Benefits to the Individual and to Society, Report prepared for the Department for Education and Employment (UK), DfEE Wider Benefits of Learning Research Centre, Institute of Education, London University, the Centre for Economic Performance, London School of Economics and the Institute for Fiscal Studies.

BYNNER, J. and EGERTON, M. (forthcoming),
The Wider Benefits of Higher Education, Report sponsored by the Higher Education Funding Council for England in Association with the Smith Institute, Department for Education and Employment (UK), DfEE Wider Benefits of Learning Research Centre, Institute of Education, London University.

CAPPELLI, P. and ROGOVSKI, N. (1994), "New Work Systems and Skills Requirements", *International Labour Review*, No. 2, pp. 205-220.

CARD, D. (1994),
"Earnings, Schooling, and Ability Revisited", NBER Working Paper No. 4832, August.

CARD, D. (1999),
"Causal Effect of Education on Earnings", in O. Ashenfelter and D. Card (eds.), *Handbook of Labor Economics*, Vol. 3A, Chapter 30, North-Holland, Amsterdam, pp. 1801-1863.

CARLINER, G. (1996),
"The Wages and Language Skills of U.S. Immigrants", NBER Working Paper No. 5793, National Bureau of Economic Research, Cambridge, MA.

CARLSON, M. (1999),
"Do Fathers Really Matter? Father Involvement and Socio-psychological Outcomes for Adolescents", Bendheim-Thoman Center for Research on Child Wellbeing, Working Paper 99-04, Princeton University.

COBB, C., HALSTEAD, T. and ROWE, J. (1996),
"If the GDP is Up, Why is America Down?", *The Atlantic Monthly*, October, pp. 59-78.

COHEN, P., STRUENING, E., MUHLIN, G., GENEVIE, E., KAPLAN, S. and PECK, H. (1982),
"Community Stressors, Mediating Conditions and Wellbeing in Urban Neighborhoods", *Journal of Community Psychology*, No. 10.

COLEMAN, J. (1988),
"Social Capital in the Creation of Human Capital", *American Journal of Sociology*, Vol. 94, Supplement, pp. S95-120.

COLEMAN, J.S. (1990),
The Foundations of Social Theory, Harvard University Press, Cambridge.

COLEMAN, J. and HOFFER, T. (1987),
Public and Private High Schools: The Impact of Communities, Basic Books, New York, pp. 94, 133-135, 231, 229 [For contrary evidence, see Stephen L. Morgan and Aage B. Sørensen (1999), "A Test of Coleman's Social Capital Explanation of School Effects", *American Sociological Review*, No. 64, pp. 661-681.]

COLEMAN, J., CAMPBELL, E., HOBSON, C., MCPARTLAND, J, MOOD, A., WEINFALL, F. and YORK, R. (1966),
Equality of Educational Opportunity, Government Printing Office, Washington, U.S.

COLLIER, P. (1998),
"Social Capital and Poverty", Working Paper, The World Bank, Washington, DC.

COUNCIL OF ECONOMIC ADVISERS (1999),
"Families and the Labor Market, 1969-1999: Analyzing the time crunch'", A Report by the CEA, Washington, DC., May.

COX, E. (2000),
in R. Putnam, R. (ed.), *Society and Civic Spirit (Gesellschaft und Gemeinsinn)*, Bertelsmann Foundation.

COX, E. and MACDONALD, D. (2000),
"Making Social Capital a Discussion Paper", New South Wales Council of Social Service.

DARLING, N. and STEINBERG, L. (1997),
"Community Influences on Adolescent Achievement and Deviance", in Brooks-Gunn, Duncan, and Aber (eds.), *Neighborhood Poverty*, Vol. II, pp. 120-131.

De HART, J. and DEKKER, P. (1999),
"Civic Engagement and Volunteering in the Netherlands: A Putnamian' Analysis", in J. Van Deth, M. Maraffi, K. Newton and P. Whiteley (eds.), *Social Capital and European Democracy*, Routledge, London, pp. 75-107.

DE LA FUENTE, A. and DOMENECH, R. (2000),
"Human Capital in Growth Regressions: How Much Difference does Data Quality Make?", CSIC, Campus de la Universidad Autonoma de Barcelona.

DOBELL, R. (2001),
"Social Capital and Social Learning in a Full World", in J.F. Helliwell (ed.), *The Contribution of Human and Social Capital to Sustained Economic Growth and Well-being: International Symposium Report*, Human Resources Development Canada and OECD.

DOUGHERTY, C. and JORGENSEN, D.W. (1996),
"International Comparisons of the Sources of Growth", *American Economic Review*, May, pp. 25-29.

DRUCKER, P. (1993),
The Post Capitalist Society, Butterworth-Heinemann, Oxford.

DURKHEIM, E. (1893),
The Division of Labor in Society, The Free Press, New York, 1984.

DURKHEIM, E. (1970),
Suicide: A Study of Sociology, Routledge and Kegan Paul Ltd, London.

EASTERLY, W. and LEVINE, R. (1997),
"Africa's Growth Tragedy: Policies and Ethnic Divisions", *Quarterly Journal of Economics*, Vol. 112(4), November, pp. 1203-1250.

ECKERSLEY, R. (1998),
Measuring Progress, Is Life Getting Better?, Commonwealth Scientific and Industrial Research Organisation Publishing, Victoria, Australia.

ELIASSON, G. (2001),
"The Role of Knowledge in Economic Growth", in J.F. Helliwell (ed.), *The Contribution of Human and Social Capital to Sustained Economic Growth and Well-being: International Symposium Report*, Human Resources Development Canada and OECD.

ENGLANDER, A.S. and GURNEY, A. (1994),
"Medium-term Determinants of OECD Productivity", *OECD Economic Studies*, No. 22, OECD, Paris.

EPSTEIN, J.L. (1995),
"School/Family/Community Partnerships: Caring for the Children we Share", Phi Delta Kappan, Vol. 76, pp. 701-712.

ERIKSON, R. and JONSSON, J. (1996),
"Explaining Class Inequality in Education: the Swedish Test Case", in R. Erikson and J.O. Jonsson (eds.), *Can Education Be Equalized?*, Westview Press, Boulder, CO.

FIELD, J. and SPENCE, L. (2000),
"Informal learning and social capital", in F. Coffield (ed.), *The Necessity of Informal Learning*, Policy Press, Bristol.

FRATIGLIONI, L., WANG, H., ERICSSON, K., MAYTAN, M. and WINBLAD, B. (2000),
"Influence of Social Network on Occurrence of Dementia: A Community-based Longitudinal Study", *The Lancet*, Vol. 355, No. 9212, 15 April.

FREEMAN, R.B., KLEINER, M.M. and OSTROGOFF, C. (1997),
"The Anatomy and Effects of Employee Involvement", Paper presented at the meeting of the American Economic Association.

FULLER, B. and CLARKE, P. (1994),
"Raising School Effects while Ignoring Culture? Local Conditions and the Influence of Classroom Tools, Rules and Pedagogy", *Review of Educational Research*, Spring, Vol. 64, No. 1, pp. 119-157.

FULLER, B. and HEYNEMAN, S. (1989),
"Third World School Quality. Current Collapse, Future Potential", *Educational Researcher*, Vol. 18(2), pp. 12-19.

FUKUYAMA, F. (1995),
Trust: The Social Virtues and the Creation of Prosperity, The Free Press, New York.

FUKUYAMA, F. (1999),
The Great Disruption: Human Nature and the Reconstitution of Social Order, The Free Press, New York.

GALLAND, O. (1999),
"Les Relations de Confiance", *La Revue Tocqueville, The Tocqueville Review*, Vol. XX, No.1.

GALLIE, D., GERSHUNY, J. and VOGLER, C. (1994),
"Unemployment, the Household and Social Networks", in Gallie *et al.* (eds.), *Social Change and the Experience of Unemployment*, Oxford University Press.

GARBARINO, J. and SHERMAN, D. (1980),
"High-Risk Neighborhoods and High-Risk Families: The Human Ecology of Child Maltreatment", *Child Development*, No. 51, pp. 188-198.

GASKIN, K. and DAVIS SMITH, J.D. (1995),
A New Civic Europe? A Study of the Extent and Role of Volunteering, The Volunteer Center, London.

GEERTZ, C. (1962),
Social Change and Economic Modernization in Two Indonesian Towns : A Case in Point, Bobbs-Merrill, Indianapolis.

GEMMELL, N. (1995),
"Endogenous Growth, the Solow Model and Human Capital", Economics of Planning, No. 28, pp. 169-183.

GEMMELL, N. (1996),
"Evaluating the Impacts of Human Capital Stocks and Accumulation on Economic Growth: Some New Evidence", Oxford Bulletin of Economics and Statistics, No. 58, pp. 9-28.

GEMMELL, N. (1997),
"Externalities to Higher Education: A Review of the New Growth Literature", Report 8 in the National Committee of Inquiry into Higher Education, Higher Education in the Learning Society, Reports 5-9, pp. 109-149.

GINGRAS, Y. and ROY, R. (1998),
"Is There a Skill Gap in Canada?", Applied Research Working Paper Series, Human Resources Development Canada.

GITTLEMAN, M. and WOLFF, E.N. (1995),
"R&D Activity and Cross-country Growth Comparisons", Cambridge Journal of Economics, Vol. 19, pp. 189-207.

GLAESER, E.L. (2001),
"The Formation of Social Capital", in J.F. Helliwell (ed.), The Contribution of Human and Social Capital to Sustained Economic Growth and Well-being: International Symposium Report, Human Resources Development Canada and OECD.

GRANOVETTER, M. (1973),
"The Strength of Weak Ties", American Journal of Sociology, No. 78, pp. 1360-1380.

GREEN, F., ASHTON, D., BURCHELL, B., DAVIES, B. and FELSTEAD, A. (1997),
"An Analysis of Changing Work Skills in Britain", Paper presented at the Analysis of Low Wage Employment Conference, Centre for Economic Performance, London School of Economics, 12-13 December.

GREEN, F., MCINTOSH, S. and VIGNOLES, A. (1999),
"Overeducation and Skills – Clarifying the Concepts", Centre for Economic Performance, Labour Market Programme Discussion Paper No. 435, London School of Economics.

GRILICHES, Z. (1996),
"Education, Human Capital, and Growth: A Personal Perspective", NBER Working Paper No. 5426, January.

GROGGER, J. (1996),
"Does School Quality Explain the Recent Black/White Wage Trend?", Journal of Labor Economics, Vol. 14(2), pp. 231-253, April.

GUISO, L., SAPIENZA, P. and ZINGALES, L. (2000),
"The Role of Social Capital in Financial Development", NBER Working Paper No. 7563, February.

GUNDLACH, E., WOSSMANN, L. and GMELIN, J. (2000),
"The Decline of Schooling Productivity in OECD Countries", Paper presented at the annual meeting of the Royal Economic Society, St Andrews, July 10-13.

HALL, P. (1999),
"Social Capital in Britain", British Journal of Political Science, No. 29, pp. 417-461.

HALL, R. and JONES, C. (1999),
"Why Do Some Countries Produce So Much More Output per Worker than Others?", Quarterly Journal of Economics, February, Vol. 114, pp. 83-116.

HALPERN, D.S. (forthcoming),
"Moral Values, Social Trust and Inequality: Can Values Explain Crime?", British Journal of Criminology, Vol. 41(2).

HALPERN, D.S. and NAZROO, J. (2000),
"The Ethnic Density Effect: Results from a National Community Survey of England and Wales", International Journal of Social Psychiatry, Vol. 46 (1), pp. 34-46.

HANIFAN, L. (1916),
"The Rural School Community Center", Annals of the American Academy of Political and Social Science, No. 67.

HANUSHEK, E.A. (1992),
"The Trade-Off between Child Quantity and Quality", Journal of Political Economy 100, No. 1, February, pp. 84-117.

HANUSHEK, E.A. (1998),
"The Evidence on Class Size", Occasional Paper No. 98-1, W. Allen Wallis Institute of Political Economy, University of Rochester, February.

HANUSHEK, E.A. and KIM, D. (1995),
"Schooling, Labor Force Quality, and Economic Growth", NBER Working Paper No. 5399, December.

HANUSHEK, E.A. and KIMKO, D.D. (2000),
"Schooling, Labor Force Quality, and the Growth of Nations", *The American Economic Review*, Vol. 90, No. 5, December.

HANUSHEK, E.A. and SOMERS, J. (1999),
"Schooling, Inequality and the Impact of Government", Paper presented for conference on Increasing Income Inequality in America, Texas A&M University, March.

HANUSHEK, E.A., KAIN, J. and RIVKIN, S. (1998),
"Teachers, Schools, and Academic Achievement", National Bureau of Economic Research Working Paper 6691, August.

HANUSHEK, E.A., KAIN, J. and RIVKIN, S. (1999),
"Do Higher Salaries Buy Better Teachers?", National Bureau of Economic Research Working Paper No. 7802, March.

HANUSHEK, E.A., RIVKIN, S. and TAYLOR, L. (1996),
"Aggregation and the Estimated Effects of School Resources", *Review of Economics and Statistics*, November, Vol. 78(4), pp. 611-627.

HANUSHEK, E., KAIN, J., MARKMAN, J. and RIVKIN, S. (2000),
"Do Peers Affect Student Achievement?", Paper prepared for the Conference on Empirics of Social Interactions, Brookings Institution, January 14-15.

HAO, L. (1994),
Kin Support, Welfare, and Out-of-Wedlock Mothers, Garland, New York.

HARBERGER, A. (1998),
"A Vision of the Growth Process", *American Economic Review*, Vol. 88, No. 1, March.

HARMON, F. and WALKER, I. (1995),
"Estimates of the Economic Return to Schooling for the United Kingdom", *American Economic Review*, No. 85, pp. 1278-1286.

HARTOG, J. (1997),
"On Returns to Education: Wandering along the Hills of ORU Land", Keynote speech for the LVIIth Conference of the Applied Econometrical Association, Maastricht, May.

HAVEMAN, R H. and WOLFE, B. (1984),
"Schooling and Economic Well-Being: The Role of Non-market Effects", *Journal of Human Resources*, No. 19, Summer, pp. 378-407.

HECKMAN, J. (1999),
"Policies to Foster Human Capital", National Bureau of Economic Research Working Paper No. 7288, Cambridge, MA, August.

HELLIWELL, J.F. (1996),
"Economic Growth and Social Capital in Asia", National Bureau of Economic Research Working Paper No. 5470, Cambridge, MA.

HELLIWELL, J.F. (2001),
"The Contribution of Human and Social Capital to Sustained Economic Growth", *The Contribution of Human and Social Capital to Sustained Economic Growth and Well-being: International Symposium Report*, Human Resources Development Canada and OECD.

HELLIWELL, J.F. and PUTNAM, R. (1999a),
"Economic Growth and Social Capital in Italy", in P. Dasgupta, and I. Serageldin (eds.), *Social Capital: a Multifaceted Perspective*, World Bank.

HELLIWELL, J.F. and PUTNAM, R. (1999b),
"Education and Social Capital", NBER Working Paper No. 7121, National Bureau of Economic Research, Cambridge, MA.

HENDERSON, A. and BERLA, N. (1994),
A New Generation of Evidence: The Family is Critical to Student Achievement, National Committee for Citizens in Education, Washington, DC.

HERS, J. (1998),
"Human Capital and Economic Growth", GPB Report, Vol. 98(2).

HESTON, A. and SUMMERS, R. (1988),
"A New Set of International Comparisons of Real Product and Price Levels Estimates for 130 Countries, 1950-1985", *Review of Income and Wealth*, XXXIV, pp. 1-26.

HESTON, A. and SUMMERS, R. (1991),
"The Penn World Table (Mark 5): An Expanded Set of International Comparisons, 1950-1988", *Quarterly Journal of Economics*, May, pp.327-368.

HIRSCHMAN, A. (1984),
"Against Parsimony: Three Easy Ways of Complicating Economic Analysis", *American Economic Review*, No. 74, pp. 88-96.

HJERRPE, R. (1998),
"Social Capital and Economic Growth", Discussion paper No. 183, Government Institute for Economic Research (VATT), November.

HO SUI-CHU, E. and WILLMS, J.D. (1996),
"The Effects of Parental Involvement on Eighth Grade Achievement", Sociology of Education, No. 69, pp. 126-141.

HODGKINSON, V. and WEITZMAN, M. (1988),
Giving and Volunteering in the United States: Findings from a National Survey, 1988 Edition, Independent Sector, Washington, D.C.

HOXBY, C. (1994),
"Do Private Schools Provide Competition for Public Schools?", National Bureau of Economic Research Working Paper 4978, New York, December.

HUMAN RESOURCES DEVELOPMENT CANADA (1999),
"The Social Context of Productivity: Challenges for Policy Makers", Speaking notes by J. Lahey for an address to the Queen's International Institute on Social Policy, August 25.

HUMPHREY, J. and SCHMITZ, H. (1998),
"Trust and Inter-firm Relations in Developing and Transition Economies", *The Journal of Development Studies*, 34(4), pp. 32-45.

INGLEHART, R. (1997),
Modernization and Postmodernization: Cultural, Economic and Political Change in 43 Societies, Princeton University Press, Princeton.

INGLEHART, R. (2000),
"Globalization and Postmodern Values", *The Washington Quarterly*, Winter.

INOGUCHI, T. (2000),
in Putnam, R. (2000b), *Society and Civic Spirit (Gesellschaft und Gemeinsinn)*, Bertelsmann Foundation.

JACOBS, J. (1961),
The Life and Death of Great American Cities, Random House, New York.

JENKINS, H. (1995a),
Education and Production in the United Kingdom, Economics Discussion Paper No. 101, Nuffield College, Oxford.

JENKINS, H. (1995b),
Infrastructure, Education and Productivity: A Multi-Country Study, DPhil thesis, Nuffield College, Oxford University.

JENSON, J. (1998),
"Mapping Social Cohesion: The State of Canadian Research", Canadian Policy Research Networks Study.

JONES, C.I. (1996),
"Human Capital, Ideas and Economic Growth", Paper presented to the VIII Villa Mondragone International Economic Seminar on Finance, Research, Education and Growth, Rome, Italy, June.

JORGENSON, D. and FRAUMENI, B. (1987),
"The Accumulation of Human and Non-human Wealth, 1948-1984", Unpublished manuscript, Harvard University.

JOSHI, H., COOKSEY, E., WIGGINS, R., MC CULLOCH, A., VERROPOULOU, G. and CLARKE, L. (1999),
"Diverse Family Living Situations and Child Development: A Multi-level Analysis Comparing Longitudinal Evidence from Britain and the United States", *International Journal of Law, Policy and the Family*, No. 13, pp. 292-314.

KAWACHI, I., KENNEDY, B.P., LOCHNER, K. and PROTHROW-STITH, D. (1997),
"Social Capital, Income Inequality, and Mortality", *American Journal of Public Health*, Vol. 87 (9), pp. 1491-1499.

KEESE, M. and PUYMOYEN, A. (forthcoming),
"Changes in Earnings Structure: Some International Comparisons Using the OECD Structure of Earnings Database", OECD Labour Market and Social Policy Occasional Papers, OECD, Paris.

KELLAGHAN, T. (1999),
"Educational Disadvantage: An Analysis", Paper presented at the Irish Department of Education and Science Conference of Inspectors, Killarney, 6-8 December.

KELLAGHAN, T., SLOANE, K., ALVAREZ, B. and BLOOM, B. (1993),
The Home Environment and School Learning. Promoting Parental Involvement in the Education of Children, Jossey-Bass, San Francisco.

KENDRICK, J. (1976),
The Formation and Stocks of Total Capital, Columbia University Press for NBER, New York.

KENKEL, D. (1991),
"Health Behavior, Health Knowledge, and Schooling", *Journal of Political Economy*, Vol. 99(2), pp. 287-305.

KENNEDY, I.B.P., LOCHNER, K. and PROTHROW-STITH, D. (1997),
"Social Capital, Income Inequality, and Mortality", *American Journal of Public Health*, Vol. 87, No. 1.

KERN, H. (1998),
"Lack of Trust, Surfeit of Trust: Some Causes of the Innovation Crisis in Germany Industry", in C. Land and R. Bachmann (eds.), *Trust within and between Organizations*, Oxford University Press, New York, pp. 203-213.

KING, R. and LEVINE, R. (1994),
"Capital Fundamentalism, Economic Development and Economic Growth", Carnegie-Rochester Series on Public Policy, No. 40.

KORBIN, J. and COULTON, C. (1997),
"Understanding the Neighborhood Context for Children and Families: Combining Epidemiological and Ethnographic Approaches", in J. Brooks-Gunn, G.J. Duncan and J.L. Aber (eds.), *Neighborhood Poverty*, Vol. II, Russell Sage Foundation, New York, pp. 65-79.

KNACK, S. (1999),
"Social Capital, Growth and Poverty; A Survey of Cross-Country Evidence", *Social Capital Initiative*, Working Paper No. 7, World Bank.

KNACK, S. (2001),
"Trust, Associational Life and Economic Performance", in J.F. Helliwell (ed.), *The Contribution of Human and Social Capital to Sustained Economic Growth and Well-being: International Symposium Report*, Human Resources Development Canada and OECD.

KNACK, S. and KEEFER, P. (1997),
"Does Social Capital Have an Economic Payoff? A Cross-Country Investigation", *Quarterly Journal of Economics*, Vol. 112(4), pp. 1251-1288.

KRUEGER, A. and LINDAHL, M. (1999),
"Education for Growth in Sweden and the World", NBER Working Paper No. 7190.

KUZNETS, S. (1962),
in *The New Republic*, Washington DC, October 20.

KYRIACOU, G. (1991),
Level and Growth Effects of Human Capital: A Cross-Country Study of the Convergence Hypothesis, C.V. Starr Centre, Working Paper No. 91-26, New York.

LA PORTA, R., LOPEZ-DE-SILANES, F., SHLEIFER, A. and VISHNY, R.W. (1997),
"Trust in Large Organisations", *American Economic Review, Papers and Proceedings*, Vol. 87(2), pp. 333-338.

LANDSBURG, S. (1993),
The Armchair Economist: Economics and Everyday Life, The Free Press, New York.

LEANA, C.R. and van BUREN, H.J. (1999),
"Organizational Social Capital and Employment Practices", *Academy of Management Review*, Vol. 24, No. 3, pp. 538-555.

LEE, J.W. and BARRO, R.J. (1997),
"Schooling Quality in a Cross-Section of Countries", NBER Working Paper, No. 6198.

LESSER, E.L. (2000),
Knowledge and Social Capital, Butterworth-Heinemann, Boston.

LEVY, F. and MURNANE, R.J. (1999),
"Are there Key Competencies Critical to Economic Success? An Economics Perspective", Paper given at the OECD Symposium on "Definition and Selection of Competencies", October.

LOURY, G. (1987),
"Why Should we Care about Group Inequality?", *Social Philosophy and Policy*, pp. 249-271.

LUCAS, R.E. (1988),
"On the Mechanisms of Economic Development", *Journal of Monetary Economics*, Vol. 22.

LUNDVALL, B.-A. and JOHNSON, B. (1994),
"The Learning Economy", *Journal of Industry Studies*, Vol. 1, No. 2, pp. 23-42.

LUNDVALL, B.-A. and MASKELL, P. (1999),
"Nation States and Economic Development: From National Systems of Production to National Systems of Knowledge Creation and Learning", in G.L. Clark *et al.* (eds.), *Handbook of Economic Geography*, Chapter 10, Oxford University Press, London.

LYNCH, J., DUE, P., MUNTANER, C. and DAVEY SMITH, G. (2001),
"Social Capital – Is it a Good Investment Strategy for Public Health", *Journal of Epidemiology and Community Health*, Vol. 54, pp. 404-408.

MADDISON, A. (1987),
"Growth and Slowdown in Advanced Capitalist Economies: Techniques of Quantitative Assessment", *Journal of Economic Literature*, No. 25, pp. 649-698.

MADDISON, A. (1991),
Dynamic Forces in Capitalist Development, Oxford University Press, Oxford.

MANKIW, N.G. (1995),
"The Growth of Nations", *Brookings Papers on Economic Activity*, No. 1, pp. 275-326.

MANKIW, N.G., ROMER, D. and WEIL, D.N. (1992),
"A Contribution to the Empirics of Economic Growth", *Quarterly Journal of Economics*, No. 107, pp. 407-437.

MCLANAHAN, S. and SANDEFUR, G.D. (1994),
Growing Up with a Single Parent: What Hurts, What Helps, Harvard University Press, Cambridge, MA.

MCMAHON, W.W. (2001),
"The Impact of Human Capital on Non-Market Outcomes and Feedbacks on Economic Development in OECD Countries", in J.F. Helliwell (ed.), *The Contribution of Human and Social Capital to Sustained Economic Growth and Well-being: International Symposium Report*, Human Resources Development Canada and OECD.

MINCER, J. (1974),
"Schooling, Experience and Earnings", National Bureau of Economic Research, Cambridge, MA.

MINGAT, A. and TAN, J. (1996),
"The Full Social Returns to Education: Estimates Based on Countries' Economic Growth Performance", Human Capital Development Papers, World Bank, Washington, DC.

MOORE, G. (1990),
"Structural Determinants of Men's and Women's Personal Networks", *American Sociological Review*, Vol. 55, October.

MOSTELLER, F. (1995),
"The Tennessee Study of Class Size in the Early School Grades", *The Future of Children* 5, No. 2, Summer/Fall, pp. 113-127.

MUNTANER, C., LYNCH, J. and SMITH, G.D. (2000),
"Social Capital and the Third Way in Public Health", *Critical public Health*, Vol. 10, No. 2.

MURNANE, R.J. (1975),
Impact of School Resources on the Learning of Inner City Children, Ballinger, Cambridge, MA.

MYERS, D. (1999),
"Close Relationships and Quality of Life", in D. Kahneman, E. Diener and E. Schwartz (eds.), *Well-being: The Foundations of Hedonic Psychology*, Russell Sage Foundation, New York.

NARAYAN, D. and PRITCHETT, L. (1998),
"Cents and Sociability: Household Income and Social Capital in Rural Tanzania", *Economic Development and Cultural Change*, World Bank, Washington.

NEHRU, V. and DHARESHWAR, A. (1994),
"New Estimates of Total Factor Productivity Growth for Developing and Industrial Countries", Policy Research Working Paper 1313, The World Bank, Washington D.C.

NEHRU, V., SWANSON, E. and DUBEY, A. (1995),
"A New Database on Human Capital Stock in Developing and Industrial Countries: Sources, Methodology and Results", *Journal of Development Economics*, No. 46, pp. 379-401.

NIE, N.H., JUNN, J. and STEHLIK-BARRY, K. (1996),
Education and Democratic Citizenship in America, University of Chicago Press, Chicago.

NONNEMAN, W. and VANHOUDT, P. (1996),
"A Further Augmentation of the Solow Model and the Empirics of Economic Growth for OECD Countries", *Quarterly Journal of Economics*, No. 111, pp. 943-953.

NORDHAUS, W. and TOBIN, J. (1972),
"Is growth obsolete?", In *Economic Growth, Fiftieth Anniversary Colloquium*, Vol. 5, NBER, New York.

NORTH, D. (1990),
Institutions, Institutional Change and Economic Performance, Cambridge University Press, New York.

NORTON, A. (1998),
"The Welfare State: Depreciating Australia's Social Capital?", *Policy*, pp. 41-43.

NYE, B. and HEDGES, L. (2000),
"The Effects of Small Classes on Academic Achievement: The Results of the Tennessee Class Size Experiment", *American Educational Research Journal*, Vol. 37, No. 1, pp. 123-151, Spring.

OECD (1976),
Measuring Social Well-being: A Progress Report on the Development of Social Indicators, Paris.

OECD (1996),
Reconciling Economy and Society: Towards a Plural Economy, Territorial Development Service, Paris.

OECD (1998),
Human Capital Investment – An International Comparison, Paris.

OECD (1999a),
Education Policy Analysis, Paris.

OECD (1999b),
Interim Report on the OECD Three-Year Project on Sustainable Development, Paris.

OECD (2000a),
Knowledge Management in the Learning Society, Paris.

OECD (2000b),
"Links between Policy and Growth: Cross-country evidence", draft paper for Working Party 1, Economics Department.

OECD (2001),
Education Policy Analysis, Paris.

OECD and Statistics Canada (2000),
Literacy in the Information Age: Final Report of the International Adult Literacy Survey, Paris.

OECD and US Department of Education (1998),
How Adults Learn, Proceedings of a conference sponsored by and held in Washington, D.C., April.

OFFE, C. and FUCHS, S. (1998),
"A Decline of Social Capital? – The German Case", in R. Putnam (2000b), *Society and Civic Spirit (Gesellschaft und Gemeinsinn)*, Bertelsmann Foundation.

OHSAKO, T. (1998),
"Learning and Social Participation by Senior Citizens in Japan: Analysis of Major Issues from an International Perspective", in *How Adults Learn*, Proceedings of a conference sponsored by OECD and the US Department of Education and held in Washington, D.C., April, 1998.

OLSON, M. (1982),
The Rise and Decline of Nations, Yale University Press, New Haven.

OMORI, T. (2001),
"Balancing Economic Growth with Well-being: Implication of the Japanese Experience", in J.F. Helliwell (ed.), *The Contribution of Human and Social Capital to Sustained Economic Growth and Well-being: International Symposium Report*, Human Resources Development Canada and OECD.

OSBERG, L. (1985),
"The Measurement of Economic Welfare," in D. Laidler (coordinator), *Approaches to Economic Well-Being*, Vol. 26 of the Research Program of the Royal Commission of the Economic Union and Development Prospects for Canada (MacDonald Commission), University of Toronto Press, Toronto.

OSBERG, L. (1992),
"Sustainable Social Development", in R.C. Allen and G. Rosenbluth (eds.), *False Promises: The Failure of Conservative Economics*, New Star Books, Vancouver, pp. 227-242.

OSBERG, L. (2001),
"Comparisons of Trends in GDP and Economic Well-being – The Impact of Social Capital", in J.F. Helliwell (ed.), *The Contribution of Human and Social Capital to Sustained Economic Growth and Well-being: International Symposium Report*, Human Resources Development Canada and OECD.

PAINTER, G. and LEVINE, D. (1999),
"Family Structure and Youths' Outcomes: Which Correlations are Causal?", Institute of Industrial Relations, Working Paper Series, No.69, September.

PEARCE, D. and ATKINSON, G. (1997),
"The Concept of Sustainable Development: An Evaluation of its Usefulness Ten Years after Bruntland", Centre for Social and Economic Research on the Global Environment, University College London and University of East Anglia.

PICCIOTTO, R. (1998),
"Gender and Social Capital", Presentation at the Gender and Development Workshop, World Bank, April (*www.worldbank.org/html/prmge/know/gendev/*).

PORTER, M. (1990),
The Competitive Advantage of Nations, The Free Press, New York.

PORTES, A. (1998),
"Social Capital: Its Origins and Applications in Modern Sociology", *Annual Review of Sociology*, No. 24, pp. 1-24.

PORTES, A. and LANDOLT, P. (1996),
"The Downside to Social Capital", *The American Prospect*, No. 26, pp. 18-21, 94, May-June.

PORTES, A. and SENSENBRENNER, J. (1993),
"Embeddedness and Immigration: Notes on the Social Determinants of Economic Action", *American Journal of Sociology*, 98(6), pp. 1320-1350.

POWELL, D.R. (1989),
"Families and Early Childhood Progams", National Association for the Education of Young Children, Washington D.C.

POWELL, W. and SMITH-DOERR, L. (1994),
"Networks and Economic Life", in N.J. Smelser and R. Swedberg (eds.), *The Handbook of Economic Sociology*, Princeton University Press, Princeton, pp 368-402.

PRITCHETT, L. (1999),
Where Has All the Education Gone?, The World Bank, Washington D.C.

PSACHAROPOULOS , G. (1994),
"Returns to Investment in Education: A Global Update", *World Development*, Vol. 22(9), pp. 1325-1343.

PUTNAM, R. (1993),
Making Democracy Work, Princeton University Press, Princeton.

PUTNAM , R.D. (1995),
"Bowling Alone: America's Declining Social Capital", *Journal of Democracy*, Vol. 6, No. 1, pp. 65-78 (*muse.jhu.edu/demo/journal_of_democracy/v006/putnam.html*).

PUTNAM, R. (2000a),
Bowling Alone: The Collapse and Revival of American Community, Simon Schuster, New York.

PUTNAM, R. (2000b),
Society and Civic Spirit (Gesellschaft und Gemeinsinn), Bertelsmann Foundation.

PUTNAM, R. (2001),
"Social Capital: Measurement and Consequences", in J.F. Helliwell (ed.), *The Contribution of Human and Social Capital to Sustained Economic Growth and Well-being: International Symposium Report*, Human Resources Development Canada and OECD.

RAUDENBUSH, S.W. and KASIM, R.M. (1998),
"Cognitive Skill and Economic Inequality: Findings from the National Adult Literacy Survey", *Harvard Educational Review*, Vol. 68 (1), pp. 33-79.

RITZEN, J. (2001),
"Social Cohesion, Public Policy, and Economic Growth: Implications for OECD Countries", in J.F. Helliwell (ed.), *The Contribution of Human and Social Capital to Sustained Economic Growth and Well-being: International Symposium Report*, Human Resources Development Canada and OECD.

RIVERA-BATIZ, F.L. (1994),
"Quantitative Literacy and the Likelihood of Employment among Young Adults in the United States", *Journal of Human Resources*, Vol. XXVII, No. 2, pp. 313-328.

RIVKIN, S.G., HANUSHEK, E.A. and KAIN, J.F. (1998),
"Teachers, Schools, and Academic Achievement", Paper presented at the annual meetings of the Econometric Society, Chicago, January.

RIZZO, J. and ZECKHAUSER, R. (1992),
"Advertising and the Price, Quantity, and Quality of Primary Care Physician Services", *Journal of Human Resources*, 27(3), pp. 381-421.

RODRIK , D. (1998),
"Where Did All the Growth Go? External Shocks, Social Conflict and Growth Collapses", NBER Working Paper, No. 6350.

RODRIK, D. (2000),
"Development Strategies for the Next Century", Paper presented at the conference on "Developing Economies in the 21st Century", Institute for Developing Economies, Japan External Trade Organization, January, 2000 (*www.ksg.harvard.edu/rodrik/devstrat.PDF*).

ROMER, P.M. (1990a),
"Human Capital and Growth: Theory and Evidence", *Carnegie-Rochester Conference Series on Public Policy*, No. 32, pp. 251-286.

ROMER, P.M. (1990b),
"Endogenous Technological Change", *Journal of Political Economy*, 98(5), Part 2, pp. 71-102.

ROSE, R. (2000),
"How Much Does Social Capital Add to Individual Health? A Survey Study of Russians", *Social Science and Medicine*, I-15 Pergamon.

ROTHSTEIN, B. (1998),
"Social Capital in the Social Democratic State – The Swedish Model and Civil Society", Department of Political Science, Göteborg University, Sweden.

ROUSE, C.E. (1998),
"Schools and Student Achievement: More Evidence from the Milwaukee Parental Choice Program", *Economic Policy Review*, March, 4(1), pp. 61-78.

RUNYAN, D., HUNTER, W. *et al.* (1998),
"Children Who Prosper in Unfavorable Environments: The Relationship to Social Capital", *Pediatrics*, 101, pp. 12-18.

SALA-I-MARTIN, X. (1997),
"I Just Ran Four Million Regressions", NBER Working Paper No. 6252.

SAMPSON, R. (1995),
"The Community", in J. Wilson and J. Petersilia (eds.), *Crime*, Institute For Contemporary Studies Press, San Francisco, pp. 193-216.

SAMPSON, R. and MORENOFF, J. (1997),
"Ecological Perspectives on the Neighborhood Context of Urban Poverty: Past and Present", in J. Brooks-Gunn, G. Duncan and J.L. Aber (eds.), *Neighborhood Poverty: Volume* II, Russell Sage Foundation, New York, pp. 1-22.

SAMPSON, R., RAUDENBUSH, S. and EARLS, F. (1997),
"Crime: A Multilevel Study of Collective Efficacy", *Science*, 277, 15 August.

SANDEFUR, G.D., MCLANAHAN, S. and WOJTKIEWICZ, R.A. (1989),
"Race and Ethnicity, Family Structure, and High School Graduation", Discussion Paper No. 893-889, Institute for Research on Poverty.

SCARPETTA, S., BASSANINI, A., PILAT, D. and SCHREYER, P. (2000),
"Economic Growth in the OECD Area: Recent Trends at the Aggregate and Sectoral Level", OECD Economics Department Working Papers No. 248.

SCHULLER, T., BYNNER, J., GREEN, A., BLACKWELL, L., HAMMOND, C. and PRESTON, J. (2001),
"Modelling and Measuring the Wider Benefits of Learning: An Initial Synthesis", Centre for Research on the Wider Benefits of Learning Institute of Education/Birkbeck College.

SEN, A. (1987),
The Standard of Living, Cambridge University Press, Cambridge.

SHIMADA, H. (1988),
"Hyu-man Uea no Keizaigaku (Economics of Humanware)", in Omori (2001), Iwanami.

SHLEIFER, A. (1998),
"State Versus Private Ownership", *Journal of Economics Perspectives*, 12 (4), pp. 133-150.

SIMONS, R. (1996),
Understanding Differences between Divorced and Intact Families: Stress, Interaction and Child Outcome, Thousand Oaks, CA, Sage.

SMITH, A. (1776),
The Wealth of Nations, Book I.

SOLOW, R.M. (1956),
"A Contribution to the Theory of Economic Growth", *Quarterly Journal of Economics*, 70, pp. 65-94.

SPENCE , A. (1973),
"Job Market Signalling", *Quarterly Journal of Economics* 87, pp. 355-374.

STEEDMAN, H. (1996),
"Measuring the Quality of Educational Outputs: A Note", Center for Economic Performance, Discussion paper No. 302, LSE.

TEACHMAN, J., PAASCH, K. and CARVER, K. (1999),
"Social Capital and the Generation of Human Capital", *Social Forces*, 75.

TEMPLE, J. (1999a),
"The New Growth Evidence", *Journal of Economic Literature*, March, 37(1), pp. 112-156.

TEMPLE , J. (1999b),
"A Positive Effect of Human Capital on Growth", *Economics Letters*, 66, pp. 131-134.

TEMPLE , J. (2001),
"Growth Effects of Education and Social Capital in the OECD", in J.F. Helliwell (ed.), *The Contribution of Human and Social Capital to Sustained Economic Growth and Well-being: International Symposium Report*, Human Resources Development Canada and OECD.

TEMPLE, J. and JOHNSON, P. (1998),
"Social Capability and Economic Growth", *Quarterly Journal of Economics*, August, pp. 965-988.

UNITED NATIONS DEVELOPMENT PROGRAMME (1990),
Human Development Report 1990, Oxford University Press, New York, NY.

UNITED NATIONS DEVELOPMENT PROGRAMME (2000),
Human Development Report 2000, Oxford University Press, New York, NY.

UZZI, B. (1996),
"The Sources and Consequences of Embeddedness for the Economic Performance of Organizations: The Network Effect", *American Sociological Review*, 61(4), pp. 674-698.

UZZI, B. (1997),
"Social Structure and Competition in Inter-firm Networks: The Paradox of Embeddedness", *Administrative Science Quarterly*, 42(1), pp. 35-67.

VAN ARK, B. and de JONG, H. (1996),
"Accounting for Economic Growth in the Netherlands since 1913", University of Groningen Research Memorandum, GD-26.

VERBA, S., SCHLOZMAN, K.L. and BRADY, H.E. (1995),
Voice and Equality: Civic Voluntarism in American Politics, Harvard University Press, Cambridge, M.A.

WEISS, A. (1995),
"Human capital vs. signalling explanations of wages", *Journal of Economic Perspectives*, 9(4), pp. 133-154.

WHITE, M. and KAUFMAN, G. (1997),
"Language Usage, Social Capital, and School Completion among Immigrants and Native-born Ethnic Groups", *Social Science Quarterly*, 78(2), pp. 385-393.

WILKINSON, R. (1996),
Unhealthy Societies: The Afflictions of Inequality, Routledge, London.

WILLMS, J.D. (1999),
"Proposal for the Measurement of Socioeconomic Status for the Focused Component of the Student Questionnaire for the OECD Programme for International Student Assessment (OECD-PISA)", The Canadian Research Institute for Social Policy (CRISP), University of New Brunswick.

WILLMS, J. D. (2001),
"Three Hypotheses about Community Effects", in J.F. Helliwell (ed.), *The Contribution of Human and Social Capital to Sustained Economic Growth and Well-being: International Symposium Report*, Human Resources Development Canada and OECD.

WOLFE, B. and HAVEMAN, R. (2001),
"Accounting for the Social and Non-market Benefits of Education", in J.F. Helliwell (ed.), *The Contribution of Human and Social Capital to Sustained Economic Growth and Well-being: International Symposium Report*, Human Resources Development Canada and OECD.

WOLFE, B.L. and ZUVEKAS, S. (1997),
Nonmarket Outcomes of Schooling, University of Wisconsin, Madison, Mimeo.

WOLFF, E.N. and M. GITTLEMAN (1993),
"The Role of Education in Productivity Convergence: Does Higher Education Matter?", in A. Szimai, B. Van Ark and D. Pilat (eds.), *Explaining Economic Growth*, Elsevier Science Publishers.

WOOLCOCK, M. (1998),
"Social Capital and Economic Development: Toward a Theoretical Synthesis and Policy Framework", Theory and Society, 27(2), pp. 151-208.

WOOLCOCK, M. (1999),
"Social Capital: The State of the Notion", Paper presented at a multidisciplinary seminar on Social Capital: Global and Local Perspectives, Helsinki, April 15.

WOOLCOCK, M. (2001),
"The Place of Social Capital in Understanding Social and Economic Outcomes", in J.F. Helliwell (ed.), *The Contribution of Human and Social Capital to Sustained Economic Growth and Well-being: International Symposium Report*, Human Resources Development Canada and OECD.

117

WORLD BANK (1998),

"The Initiative on Defining, Monitoring and Measuring Social Capital Text of Proposals Approved for Funding", Environmentally and Socially Sustainable Development Network, Social Capital Initiative, Working Paper No. 2, June.

WORMS, J.P. (1998a),

"Old and New Civic and Social Ties in France", in Putnam (2000b).

WORMS, J.P. (1998b),

"La crise du lien social, le problème du chaînon manquant", Empan, No. 32, December 1998, pp. 94-104.

WORMS, J.P. (2000),

"Old and New Civic and Social Ties in France", in R. Putnam (ed.), Society and Civic Spirit (Gesellschaft und Gemeinsinn), Bertelsmann Foundation.

WOSSMANN, L. (2000),

"Schooling Resources, Educational Institutions and Student Performance: The International Evidence", Kiel Working Paper No. 983, May.

YANKELOVICH, D. (1981),

New Rules: Searching for Self-fulfillment in a World Turned Upside Down, Bantam Books, New York.

OECD PUBLICATIONS, 2, rue André-Pascal, 75775 PARIS CEDEX 16
PRINTED IN FRANCE
(96 2001 01 1 P) ISBN 92-64-18589-5 – No. 51647 2001